RAILWAY
MODELLING SKILLS

RAILWAY
MODELLING SKILLS

Peter Marriott

THE CROWOOD PRESS

First published in 2015 by
The Crowood Press Ltd
Ramsbury, Marlborough
Wiltshire SN8 2HR

www.crowood.com

British Library Cataloguing-in-Publication Data
A catalogue record for this book is available from the British Library.

ISBN 978 1 84797 955 1

Disclaimer
The author and the publisher do not accept any responsibility in
any manner whatsoever for any error or omission, or any loss,
damage, injury, adverse outcome, or liability of any kind incurred
as a result of the use of any of the information contained in this
book, or reliance upon it. If in doubt about any aspect of railway
modelling skills and techniques, readers are advised to seek
professional advice.

Frontispiece supplied by Chris Nevard/*Model Rail*

Designed and typeset by Guy Croton
Publishing Services, Tonbridge, Kent

Printed and bound in Malaysia by Times Offset (M) Sdn Bhd

CONTENTS

ACKNOWLEDGEMENTS

Thanks go to the numerous people who have made railway modelling a more enjoyable place for me, including David Aldis, David Brown, Bill Carmen, John Emerson, Ian Futers, Stewart Gorman, Stephan Kraus, Chris Leigh, Martyn Rees, Pelle Søeborg, Rob Spendelow and Colin Tucker.

Thanks go to my wife Mary, who sometimes has to put up with living with model railways dotted around our house. I really do appreciate her patience and long suffering!

Thanks also go to the photographers and model makers who agreed for me to use some of their pictures in this book:

• Stephan Kraus, who is a professional layout builder in Germany offering diorama and layout building services plus modelling seminars at www.modell-bau-smk.de.
• Chris Nevard, as *Model Rail*'s ace photographer, who always brings out the best in my layouts through his photographic expertise.
• Paul Marshall-Potter, whose recent joint DVD production with Paul Lunn will be inspirational to many would-be layout builders.

• Busch and its agents in the UK, Golden Valley Hobbies, for the pictures of their diminutive Feldbahn system.

In addition, I say thank you to model railway editors who have published words and pictures about my layouts over the past decade and who have agreed that snippets of those layouts that have appeared in their magazines are portrayed within this book:

• Dennis Lovatt as editor of *Bachmann Times*, who suggested that I build a tiny layout to convey the impression of four miniature railways.
• Ben Jones, now of *British Railway Modelling*, who has published numerous articles about my European layouts during his spell at *Model Rail* magazine.
• Richard Foster as editor of *Model Rail*, who continues to pour over my words and pictures each month and turns them into something that looks better in the magazine.
• Andrew Burnham of the *Continental Modeller* for featuring my European layouts.

The DMU washing plant by Scenecraft with a modified Hornby Class 110 DMU repainted in Mexican Bean colours as it ran on the West Highland Line.

CHAPTER ONE

SKILLS, WHAT SKILLS?

*A skill is a learned ability to carry out a task with results within time
and energy using tools and materials.*

HOW TO LEARN NEW SKILLS

Railway modellers can become very skilful in various disciplines. Many of them do not realize that they have learned do so much until they are asked what they have accomplished in the hobby. Far from putting people off from joining in the hobby, the various skills should open up their minds to the wide array of things that may be learned and enjoyed as a railway modeller. The hobby can be very satisfying and most of the skills are quite easy to pick up and are fun to learn.

Different skills will appeal to some people more than others, but if there is something we really do not want to learn we can usually get other people to do those tasks for us. The hobby has become so varied and comprehensive that there are many individuals and small firms offering their services in a number of areas. There are also products that give us shortcuts to learning a skill, which is particularly important in today's society where time is at a premium.

From time to time, it is a good idea to make a list of our personal skills. This may help us to realize that we may like to improve some aspects of our modelling, while being content with our other skills. Modellers set themselves the challenge of improving their skills, which is a good way of freshening up the hobby if they find they are stuck in a modelling

With the arrival of resin buildings, the modeller can choose to buy suitable buildings for his layout and simply fix them to the baseboard. But there are some quick and easy skills that can be learned to turn resin buildings into something more distinctive, including painting parts of them, adding curtains, adding signs and weathering them. Here the three middle houses are identical, but by painting the front doors different colours and by adding different curtains the row of houses has been personalized.

Railway modellers are well blessed for research material to make their model railways more realistic. Here just three books about the Wisbech and Upwell Tramway demonstrate that information is readily available. Even if books are out of print, there is a steady exchange of them through avenues such as auction sites and Amazon. In addition to books, there are DVDs, YouTube videos, magazine articles and specialist societies supplying words and pictures about almost every railway line that has ever operated in the UK. Successful research is a skill that can soon be picked up.

rut. The more I think about the hobby, the more I conclude that knowing what you want from a model railway is the key to getting and improving the main skills required. If you know what you enjoy most in the hobby, you will find learning more about how to do certain tasks a pleasure rather than a necessary task to be undertaken.

There are various ways to improve railway modelling skills. These include attending training courses that are run on a variety of topics, such as airbrushing, baseboard construction, tracklaying, scenery making and much more. Books, bookazines and magazines increasingly feature 'how to' articles containing a series of photos following a construction project. The best of these include lists of tools and materials and explicit pictures and captions so that the reader is left in no doubt as to how to accomplish a specific task. The hobby is also now blessed with a huge number of DVDs, demonstrating various skills and techniques, that we can watch in our living room or on the PC. These are available from UK and overseas sources, which broadens the scope of the expertise demonstrated.

The huge number of model railway exhibitions throughout the country gives us ample opportunity to ask questions of other modellers about how they did such and such. Some exhibitions arrange for demonstration stands and lectures with experts in a particular field, thus passing on their learned wisdom.

Wharfedale Road is an OO-scale compact layout that is suitable for the steam or diesel eras.
PAUL MARSHALL-POTTER

Joining a model railway club and learning as the club builds its own layouts is another way forward. Fellow club members will be only too happy to help you improve your skills as you work on the layout together. Another option is to join a model railway forum and post your questions for other members to offer their words of experience.

Look at previously published magazine articles to see if the subject that you want to learn about has already been discussed before. For example, to search the index of published articles in *Model Rail* magazine go to: www.ukmodelshops.co.uk/ModelRail

HOW TO GET THE MOST OUT OF THIS BOOK

The purpose of this book is to:

• Make the hobby as appealing and enjoyable as possible.
• Provide some guidelines as to what products and projects will provide satisfaction.
• Explain the many techniques that can be learned and the tools and materials that will be needed for those tasks.

Some skills are trial and error. Just how much diluted weathering dye is needed to weather this plastic portaloo? Only by trying various mixes of weathering dye and seeing how the plastic portaloo takes the dye will the modeller learn about weathering skills.

The choice of models, scales, scenery materials, accessories and so on available to railway modellers today is huge. There are a good number of large and small manufacturers producing everything the modeller could want on his layout. This picture shows just one corner of a well-stocked model shop (Model Junction in Slough).

An OO-scale Sealion wagon weathered by Danish modeller Pelle Søeborg. Weathering is one of the newer skills in the hobby and there are plenty of books and DVDs that demonstrate how to do it well.

- Show how it has never been easier to make a good-looking model railway layout that you can be proud of.

This book is written for those who like running trains, but also want to expand and improve their layout over time. They want to feel more confident over a wider range of model railway skills and perhaps want to gain the confidence to tackle modelling tasks that they have shied away from before.

When I began modelling railways I read model railway magazines, but found that rarely did the articles on layout building say how such and such a task was performed, or what products were used. I have therefore set out to be comprehensive in the information this book provides, with the ultimate aim that even if I have not described the specific task you want to do, by the end of the book you will have gained sufficient knowledge to know how to set about the task.

OVERLEAF: *Even a single line can offer interesting scenic opportunities such as this GWR branch line modelled for a* **Model Rail** *publication.*
CHRIS NEVARD/MODEL RAIL

The Main Skills Needed for the Successful Building of a Model Railway

Deciding what you want out of a model railway
The pleasure you gain from the hobby depends very much upon how much you 'love' the model that you are building. This highlights the need to think carefully about what you like most about railway modelling before starting to build your 'dream' layout.

Knowing what tools are available Tools for making model railways are a mixture of domestic tools and those sold by specialist shops in the hobby world. For example, when detailing locomotives a craft knife, micro-paintbrushes, small files, a pick and place tool, small screwdrivers, a small drill and tweezers will all make the tasks so much easier. If you have these tools to hand before starting a project the work will be quicker, more effective and less frustrating.

Designing a layout Some in the hobby never get past the notepad and pencil stage, but the keener you are to model a location, the quicker you will be building that

Craft knives and packs of brushes are available quite cheaply from hobby stores. These two packs cost less than £9.

layout. The key here is to know what layout will give you the most enjoyment and build that one.

Researching the prototype Railway history, geography and technology are absorbing parts of our hobby. Successfully researching a topic generally means that the finished product will be more accurate, the builder will get more satisfaction from his project and the longer he will stay a railway modeller.

Building the baseboard Good baseboards are the essential foundation of a layout. Build a good baseboard and this will help with the tracklaying process and the running of the trains. Make a bad baseboard and you might end up leaving the hobby through frustration. If you have doubts about your ability to construct a good baseboard, there are many firms that will be keen to build one for you.

Laying the track This is a very important skill, because well-laid track can definitely contribute to enjoyment in the hobby. Conversely, poorly laid track can result in derailments and annoyance. Time spent laying track well will be rewarded many times over. If you do not feel confident about laying track, you might consider using sectional track instead of flexible track, which, if ballasted and weathered nicely, can look realistic.

Ballasting and weathering the track This can greatly improve the finished look of a layout. Well-ballasted and weathered track elevates the look of a layout. Even 'train set' track can be made to look very realistic with a little care. These are skills that can be learned before working on your layout and time spent on the learning process will never be wasted.

Wiring and point control Some modellers like wiring, others do not. The wiring on layouts can be kept simple, while still working effectively. There is plenty of published advice on correctly wiring a layout and DCC has potentially simplified the wiring required for isolated track in such locations as locomotive depots.

Train control With DCC, modellers have a huge range of control possibilities from which to choose. It is not as difficult to learn DCC as some would think and it is definitely worth weighing up all the advantages and disadvantages before deciding whether to use the older analog DC (Direct Current) method of control or to 'go DCC'. It will, of course, be much cheaper to buy one type of control system rather than start with one system and then change to the other.

Soldering This is important for wiring up the track and adding electrical accessories, but can be largely ignored for the rest of the hobby unless you wish to make metal kits of carriages, locomotives, wagons, signals and other accessories. So a basic knowledge may suffice, or you may choose to learn the skill in more detail to enable you to build metal kits.

Making the landscape Many modellers know the time-served methods of making the landscape, but there are now a number of time- and weight-saving methods that are quick to learn and economical to do. These include using pieces of roof insulation hard foam for the landscape foundations.

General scenery Never before in the hobby has there been such a good selection of scenic materials available. Learn how to use them properly and you will soon be building a layout with better scenery than you imagined possible.

Building the platforms This really is not that difficult and should not take too much time, but it transforms a layout. The few key skills needed to build platforms are measuring, cutting cardboard, gluing card together and painting, including a white line.

Adding buildings There is a range of skills, including using the right building, making it or buying something similar to what you'd really like, as well as where and how to 'plant' the building on the layout. Today, the modeller is faced with the choice of using ready-made resin buildings, or kits made from cardboard, laser-cut card, laser-cut timber or plastic.

We just love watching trains move. Here at the Nuremberg Toy Fair the locomotive captivates the eyes of passers-by.

Adding the details Many modellers find this to be one of the best parts of the hobby. It can be a lot of fun and the more you know about what is available for your layout, the more you can fine-tune the layout to meet your preferences. A huge range of figures, accessories and more is available in all the popular scales.

Finishing the layout Some say that layouts are never finished and there are indeed always improvement and detailing projects that can be done. The skill here is knowing when enough is enough. Too many details can turn a model railway into a train set.

Operating a layout How we run our trains is very much a personal matter. Some just like to 'play trains', while others work up prototypical timetables for their layout that they, and possibly their friends, stick to precisely in operating sessions.

Exhibiting a layout Many modellers like to exhibit their handiwork to others at model railway shows. There are things that can be learned that make exhibiting a layout less stressful and more fun. Layout exhibitors go a long way to ensuring that modellers continue to gain enthusiasm for the hobby.

DEMONSTRATION SEQUENCE

Making rock faces is quite an easy skill to learn and there are various learning kits available to show you how to do it. Woodland Scenics is a company that has a good range, including one featuring making rocks.

Painting rock pieces is one of those skills that is quickly learned. It is always fun to learn new techniques. It injects enthusiasm into our modelling time if we do not always stick to our long-established methods.

This small rock face took a couple of hours to make and to bed into the scenery.

The segment turntable by Noch is a good space-saving way to reduce the length of a layout.
CHRIS NEVARD/MODEL RAIL

Because of the scope of the modelling tasks in the hobby, we will cover a number of skills. Some of these skills cross over, so, for example, painting needs to be done on rolling stock, buildings, the track, roads and much more. It may be good to look at Chapter 2 on tools first because there the tools are recommended that experience has shown to be most useful in the hobby.

We work through many modelling projects to demonstrate the simplest but most effective techniques and materials. The book has been prepared as a work of reference supplying suggested lists of materials and tools so that you can 'stock up' on the materials before you commence a project. The aim of each project is to give you confidence that you will be able to undertake such a project quickly so as to add to your modelling enjoyment.

When I began writing this book, I was anticipating that it would cover all aspects of railway modelling skills, but after a few months I realized that one book could not contain all that information unless it ran in excess of 500 pages. I decided therefore to concentrate on the more modern aspects of railway modelling on the basis that there is already a goodly amount of published information readily available on matters such as wiring a layout, using point motors and traditional train control. Instead, I have included recent modern techniques such as the use of hard foam in making a baseboard, the latest scenery-making techniques, DCC (Digital Command Control) train control, laser-cut kits, downloadable kits and hopefully many more tips to interest the reader. I do hope that you find some ideas in this book for your current and future layouts.

CHAPTER TWO

THE TOOLS YOU WILL NEED

Just knowing what tools are available can be a good way to improve your skills.

The basic tools that will be needed to make a layout are both readily available and inexpensive. Most of us have a large DIY store near to our home and we may well already have some of the necessary tools in our shed or garage. Some of these tools are specifically made for the modeller, whilst others have other primary uses, but can be useful for railway modellers too. Having the right tools makes modelling easier, quicker and more successful. Tools generally last a long while and we get so familiar with them that we don't even think about them – but we would be lost without them.

Tool suppliers regularly attend the larger model railway exhibitions. Suppliers include: Squires (www.squirestools.com); Eileen's Emporium (www.eileensemporium.com); Expo Tools (www.expo-tools.com) and more. Gaugemaster retails its own expanding brand of tools (www.gaugemaster.com) and Hobbycraft stores carry a good range of tools (www.hobbycraft.co.uk).

Health warning Remember that all tools can be dangerous. Store them and use them well out of reach of children and pets. Do not leave them where folks can trip over them. Wear protective eye protection and other clothing as recommended by the manufacturer. When working with adhesives or paint, keep the room well ventilated.

The basic tools for making baseboards include a rechargeable electric drill, set square, saw, pencil for marking out, steel ruler, paintbrush for the PVA adhesive, a surform and a screwdriver.

Clamps are very useful tools. Either made from plastic or metal, they perform valuable functions holding parts of kits in position while the adhesive sets, holding backscenes in position, holding the timber of a baseboard together as the adhesive dries and other tasks where an extra pair of hands is invaluable.

CLAMPS

Small plastic spring clamps are a real boon for kit building. Whilst assembling parts, they can be used to hold two or more pieces together as the glue sets. These can be bought very cheaply at model railway shows from various companies, with some of the clamps retailing at less than £1 each. Metal G clamps are also available for heavier duty tasks, such as holding together baseboard parts while the adhesive dries.

Useful for: Holding in position temporary back scenes, holding together parts of kits while the adhesive dries and holding baseboard parts together while the adhesive dries

Supplier: They can be bought at model railway shows and from specialist suppliers.

COFFEE STIRRERS OR ICED-LOLLY STICKS

Stirrers can be used to make fences for level crossings and anywhere else that real wood can be used on a layout. Some materials used scenically on a layout do not take kindly to being dragged along with a paintbrush or metal tool, such as Woodland Scenics Realistic Water. To 'handle' such viscous fluids it is recommended that a small wooden stick be used for this.

Useful for: Dragging resin-based water fluid to the edge of a water feature, shaping rock faces as the rock moulding plaster sets, stirring paint.

Supplier: Your favourite iced lolly! Alternatively, various scenic manufacturers supply them in their scenery kits. Of course, coffee shops usually have a jar full of them near to their checkout, so when you buy your next coffee remember to save your stirrer!

CRAFT KNIFE

One of the staples of modelling tasks is the craft knife. These need fresh new blades for every new modelling task, because a new blade cuts cleanly and quickly and is much less frustrating than a blade that snags whilst it cuts. Poor blades increase the time taken to do anything, because it might mean that the same job has to be done twice if the first job was not good enough.

Useful for: Cutting cardboard and plastic card of all shapes and sizes. Working on locomotive detailing and modification projects, laying flexible track and much more. At least one of these is an essential item in the toolbox, plus some spare blades.

Supplier: Art shops, DIY stores, stationers, hardware stores, Hobbycraft, model shops and specialist tool suppliers and at model railway shows.

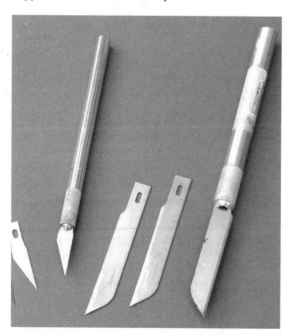

To the left is a standard craft knife with spare blades and to the right is a Woodland Scenics Foam Knife with its longer blades, which are good for cutting through hard foam. As with all craft knifes, have plenty of spare new blades in stock because blunt blades are time-consuming to work with and they will make it very difficult to achieve good results.

FILES

A set of small files is useful for a number of tasks ranging from tracklaying, remedying any small moulding faults on figures and accessories, as well as reducing the size of buffer-beam pipes so that they will fit in the small holes on the buffer beam when detailing locomotives.

Useful for: Smoothing the edges of cut rail when laying track. Removing excess burr on metal or plastic kits. Detailing locomotives.

Supplier: DIY stores, hardware stores, Hobbycraft, model shops and specialist tool suppliers at model railway shows.

Needle and small files are essential for working with flexible track – where the rail is cut the edges may be jagged, which could cause derailments and cut fingers. Small files are also useful for removing burr from kit parts and when adding detailing parts to locomotives.

FIBREGLASS BRUSH

To clean the top and sides of the moving rails on the points that have been weathered or to get into small spaces, there is little to touch the cleaning ability of a fibreglass brush. It works on the same principle as a propelling pencil and so enables the fibres to be pushed out as demanded. I find that these tools can be useful too for cleaning fine burr from plastic or metal parts of kits. They are also good for scratching (distressing) the sides of wagons and imitation steel girder bridges and so on to give a well-worn look.

Health warning Do not touch the ends of the fibreglass bristles because they can easily get stuck into one's fingers, causing irritation.

Useful for: Cleaning the points after weathering. Also a good weathering tool in itself and for removing fine blemishes on kits and other models.

Supplier: Specialist tool suppliers and at model railway shows.

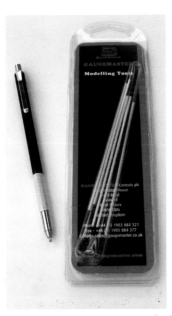

A fibreglass retractable brush is excellent for track cleaning (particularly on the moving parts of the points) and distressing wagons. Refills are available and the brushes are sold in various thicknesses.

HAMMER

We have generally got a hammer or two in the garage or the shed. For making baseboards, domestic hammers are useful, but for modelling tasks, such as knocking in track pins, the smaller craft hammers or even toffee hammers are useful.

Useful for: Baseboard construction and knocking in track pins

Supplier: DIY stores, hardware shops, large supermarkets and specialist tool suppliers.

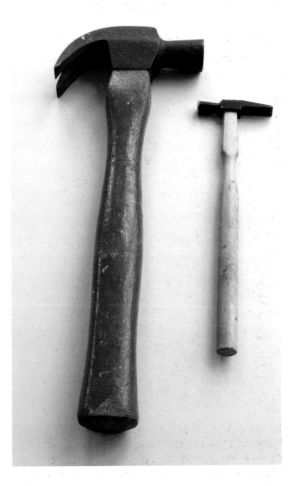

The larger hammer is useful for making a baseboard, but the smaller craft hammer is best for working with track pins where the much smaller head will fit through the rails.

MICRO-PAINTBRUSHES

Sometimes even the smallest paintbrush seems too large for the finest painting job. These tiny brushes feature a bendable bristle brush. They are sold in two types – with the familiar bristle head and almost a pom-pom of tiny fibres to form a rounder head to the brush. These brushes (they are called 'applicators' on the packets) can easily be bent to any angle. I have tried them with paint on small areas and found them to be very useful. They will also be suitable for the placement of small controlled amounts of material, such as adhesive, lubricant and solvent when modifying locomotive detailing. They come in regular, fine and superfine sized heads.

Useful for: Ideal for all scales. A great, cheap way of applying a small amount of paint. Very versatile for locomotive detailing and fine painting.

Supplier: Available in the UK from www.modeljunction.info and other retailers.

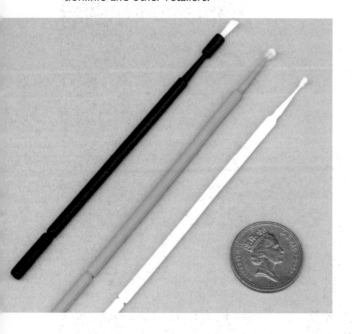

Three micro-paintbrushes with different heads. The plastic handles of these brushes are flexible and can be bent to get into difficult corners. Such brushes are ideal for fine painting on rolling stock, figures and buildings.

MINI-DRILL

Mini-drills are made by a number of companies. Most are mains-powered, but some are rechargeable. They are useful when making a baseboard, but also when adding details to the layout and modifying rolling stock. A set of different sized drills is also needed.

Useful for: Drilling holes in the baseboard to take wires, making holes to take fence posts, telegraph posts, railway signs and so on. Drilling out small holes in locomotives to take buffer-beam details, air pipes and so on.

Supplier: Available from model shops, specialist suppliers and some hobby shops.

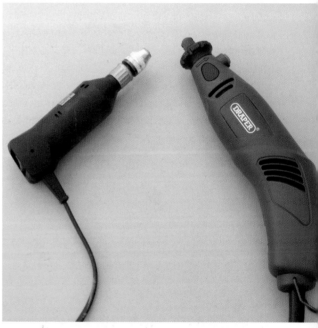

Electric mini-drills are important in a modeller's toolkit for drilling holes in the baseboard to take signal posts, telegraph poles and traffic signs. They are also good for drilling small holes in locomotive buffer beams to add parts and to take wire handrails.

PAINTBRUSHES

One can never have too many paintbrushes. Because they do wear out after a time, it is always worth having a few replacements in stock. Flat brushes are good for painting the larger areas, whilst pinpoint brushes are best for finer work. There is no need to buy expensive paintbrushes if the work is to cover large areas, such as the base colour of the scenery, or painting the grey of a road. Good-quality brushes are important for painting fine detail, such as the detail on figures.

Useful for: Applying adhesive and painting the landscape, roads, platforms and buildings. Painting loco details and figures. Can also be used in the weathering process on buildings, bridges, wagons and rolling stock.

Supplier: Art shops, some supermarkets and specialist tool suppliers at model railway shows.

PICK AND PLACE TOOL

This is a tool like a pen with a small sticky tip on the end that is useful for picking up and placing small parts such as locomotive details. To regain the sticky tension on the point, just roll the tip on adhesive tape.

Useful for: Picking up detail parts when they are fiddly, such as locomotive details.

Supplier: Available from Gaugemaster and others.

PLASTIC SYRINGE

A plastic syringe is very handy for dispensing a controlled amount of liquid. When the fluid is diluted (for example, PVA glue), this assists the smooth flow of the fluid from the tool. Deluxe Materials retail a Pin Point Syringe Kit that includes two syringes and three sizes of stainless-steel tips. Wash the tip of the

A selection of paintbrushes, Woodland Scenics T-Pins plus a wooden stick similar to a coffee stirrer or iced-lolly stick that are useful for a multitude of small jobs, such as working with water fluids and sculpting rock faces.

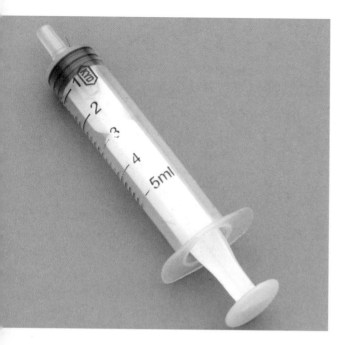

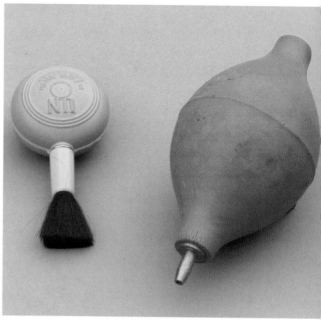

A plastic syringe can be very useful for dispensing diluted PVA for ballasting and scenic work. It is useful also for carefully pouring water fluids, such as resin-based liquids. Practise pushing the plunger slowly and steadily until you feel confident working with it.

To the left is a photographic puffer bottle for removing dust from a camera lens and to the right is a larger rubber-based puffer bottle that works very well blowing away dust and excess scenic materials. Both are good when cleaning debris from a layout and especially when taking photographs of your layout and rolling stock.

bottle or pipette after each use to ensure that the tool stays free of hardened glue.

Useful for: Applying PVA (diluted) on to ballast or scenic areas. Applying water materials (such as Woodland Scenics Realistic Water or Deluxe Materials Scenic Water) in confined areas such as streams or small puddles.

Supplier: Deluxe Materials, Hobbycraft and specialist tool suppliers at model railway shows.

PUFFER

Using a puffer is a great way to rid the layout, a building or an item of rolling stock of stray scenic material, dust or static grass fibres. It is also very useful when you are taking photographs of a layout and rolling stock.

Useful for: Blowing away dust and excess scenery materials. Preparing the layout and rolling stock for a photographic shoot.

Supplier: Specialist tool suppliers at model railway shows and photographic shops.

SCREWDRIVERS

We all have a number of screwdrivers at home. Some have flat blades, some are of the Phillips cross-head type. Some are small; others are large. For making baseboards, the domestic sized screwdrivers are useful. For modelling tasks, smaller screwdrivers are preferable, for example when dismantling items of rolling stock.

Useful for: Baseboard construction, disassembling and reassembling locomotives and road vehicles.

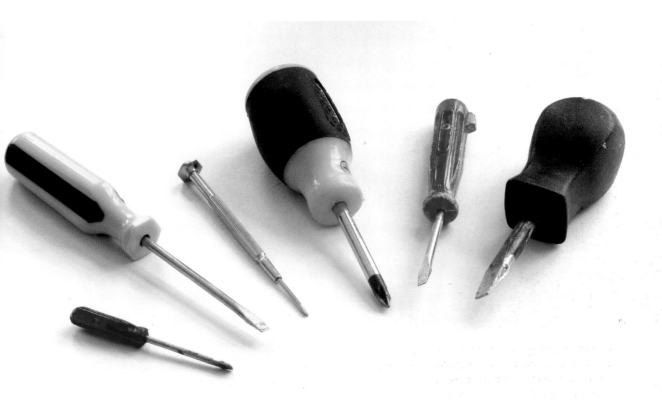

A selection of screwdrivers for an enormous number of tasks, from building the baseboard to reassembling a locomotive. Should its blades become damaged, it is best to dispose of the screwdriver because it will never work well again.

Supplier: DIY stores, hardware shops, large supermarkets and specialist tool suppliers.

SELF-SEALING CUTTING BOARD

Get the largest cutting board that you can accommodate on your workbench so that you may be able to cut cardboard or plastic card in one cut rather than two sweeps of the blade. These are one of the workbench essentials for scratch-building platforms and buildings, when making kits and generally as protection for the desk or table.

Useful for: Cutting cardboard, wood and plastic. Also useful when cutting the parts from sprues of kits of all types of material.

Supplier: Art shops, hardware shops and specialist tool suppliers at model railway shows.

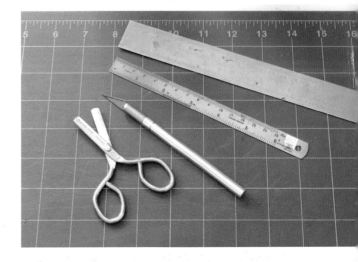

A self-sealing cutting board is essential for any form of kit making because it protects the desk or workbench. Steel rulers are necessary when cutting most materials and a small pair of cheap scissors is suitable for cutting stray pieces of scenery fibres and foliage.

STEEL RULER

A steel ruler is recommended rather than one made from plastic or wood, because the blade of a sharp craft knife will not cut into a steel ruler. It is essential when cutting cardboard, plastic or wood. Go for a 30cm (12in) ruler rather than a 15cm (6in) one when needing to cut larger pieces.

Useful for: When cutting cardboard, laser-cut kits and plastic of all shapes and sizes.

Supplier: Art shops, hardware shops, DIY stores and specialist tool suppliers at model railway shows.

T-PINS

These packs of Woodland Scenics T-shaped metal pins are around 5cm (2in) long. They are really useful for holding together scenery as the adhesive sets and for supporting trees and other accessories as they are being fixed into the landscape.

Useful for: Supporting trees, fence posts and other items whilst the adhesive holding them is drying and for holding hard foam scenery in place whilst the glue dries.

Supplier: Woodland Scenics; for dealers, see www.bachmann.co.uk.

TWEEZERS

What would we do without tweezers? They are good for holding figures and accessories as we add details to our layouts. They are useful for pushing signs into place on buildings, placing fence posts in drilled holes in the baseboard and picking up and sliding locomotive numbers into place. They can be bought singly, or in packs with a variety of types of tweezers.

Useful for: Holding fine accessories whilst positioning them. Handling figures, signs, detailing parts, fence posts and much more.

Supplier: Some hardware stores or specialist tool suppliers at model railway shows.

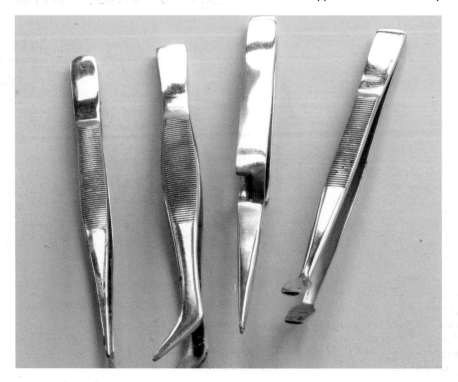

This set of tweezers cost less than £3 from a model railway show, but has served me well on numerous tasks over a decade or more. If you get dried glue on the tweezers, pour on boiling hot water to remove it.

STORAGE BOXES

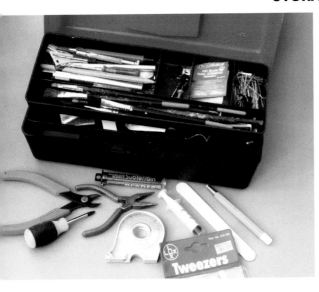

It is worth buying a plastic toolbox in which to store all your tools. There is nothing more frustrating than having to search for tools and by the time you have found the required tools for a task your enthusiasm for the modelling may well have disappeared.

There are many plastic storage boxes available for storing scenic materials such as static grass fibres. This storage box has nine large trays, plus there are additional smaller storage compartments in the lid. Because these are made from plastic they are easy to move around the house or garage, or take to model railway shows.

A small plastic box with a lid is a good way to store track bits and pieces such as track pins, fishplates, spare wheels and couplings. These boxes can be stacked on top of one another and are also suitable for storing road vehicles, figures and detailing accessories.

A close-up of a plastic box with track bits. These plastic boxes are light in weight and are available from hobby stores, DIY stores and discount shops.

CHAPTER THREE

HOW TO DESIGN A NEW LAYOUT

Designing a layout to meet most of your needs ensures satisfaction in the hobby.

Some of us build new layouts at regular intervals, whilst others are happy to build just one new layout every decade, or even one layout in a lifetime. One modeller may already know the design and track requirements for their next layout, but others of us are constantly looking around for new design ideas.

HOW DO I GET IDEAS?

Layout designing is a fascinating part of the hobby. If you like sketching track plans on bits of paper you will know what I mean. If you are not one of those who like thinking up plans, there are a number of places to look for inspiration, including the many track-planning books. In Appendix I, several recommended books are listed to show just some of the available selection. Peco's track-plan booklets feature many of the famous plans by C.J. Freezer and these are still a source of inspiration. The Peco Setrack booklets are available for N and OO scale and provide a good selection of track plans.

Using true to scale paper templates of track pieces from Peco enables a modeller to see exactly which pieces of track are needed. These full-size templates can be photocopied and cut out for positioning on a baseboard to see exactly what track can be accommodated on your baseboards. These templates can be downloaded from the Peco website at www.peco-uk.com.

Wharfedale Road is an OO-scale compact layout built especially for the Right Track DVD Layout Planning and Design. It shows that can be achieved by using mainly 'off the peg' products. For more information go to: www.model-railway-dvd.co.uk/right_track19.php. PAUL MARSHALL-POTTER

The first steps of a new layout are quite exciting. Peco paper-point templates are being used with pieces of sectional track to experiment with a new layout design. This will help to determine whether the plan on paper will work in reality.

Hornby's quarter-scale plastic track pieces are a useful way to lay out the track plan to see exactly how it will look full size. These pieces can be used over and over again. For more information see www.hornby.com. Hornby also produces a TrakMat that measures 180 x 120cm (71 x 47in) for use by beginners. Roco used to make scale replicas of its HO RocoLine track pieces that could be cut out from a main template and fixed to a lined piece of shiny thick card.

There are websites with track plans for our enjoyment. These include www.freetrackplans.com. A US Internet forum that has a huge number of good ideas on layout design is the Layout Design Special Interest Group, whose purpose is to aid efforts to design and create layouts to achieve an owner's layout goals. The Group acts as a forum for members' exchange of information and ideas. It promotes, develops, supports and encourages participation by the public in model railways. The Group's website is worth looking at: www.ldsig.org.

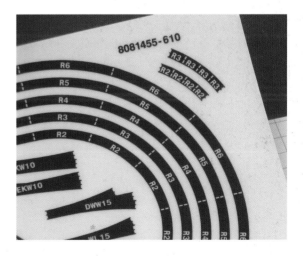

Roco used to produce miniature track templates for its various sectional pieces of track, which could be positioned on a scale baseboard to ensure that a track plan was workable. Remember that it is always best to leave sufficient room around the edge of the track for scenic work. Track sitting on the edge of a baseboard can lead to locomotives falling off the edge of a layout.

Model Railroader magazine's annual *Model Railroad Planning* bookazine published by Kalmbach from the USA describes the design and construction of various layouts in N to O scales. Some of the plans within the magazine are large US-style basement style layouts, but others are compact layout plans (which could be adapted for UK or European layouts), plus tips on layout construction. Do not be put off that this is a US-based publication – most UK modellers will find something of interest. These are available in the larger WHSmith stores, but also at www.spv.co.uk.

A good demonstration of layout design and layout building is the Wharfedale Road layout built specifically for the RightTrack DVD no.19, Layout Planning and Design. The DVD shows the changes that the design went through, as well as different interpretations of the same track plan, to provide inspiration and encouragement for the viewer.

USING TECHNOLOGY

Model railway planning programmes for use on PCs are available from various companies, including: Anyrail (www.anyrail.com/index_en.html); Winrail (www.winrail.com); www.trackplanning.com; and www.templot.com. Some of these websites enable you to try their programmes before purchasing the whole package.

To design compact layouts there are several really useful websites that include: www.wymann.info/ShuntingPuzzles/index.html and www.carendt.com. There are also several companies offering to design and build a layout for you. These include Professional Layout Design (www.pls-layouts.co.uk) and Elite Baseboards (www.elitebaseboards.net).

Hornby's Virtual Model Railway CD-ROM is a comprehensive design program enabling the user to design and plan layouts in both 2D and 3D. To see a layout virtually before you build it, TrainPlayer is a US-based program that has UK stock and can import files from AnyRail so that the layout you design can be converted into a working virtual layout. For more information, go to www.trainplayer.com or www.elitebaseboards.net/layout-construction-services.

WHAT DO YOU NEED TO THINK ABOUT?

Each time you begin to make a new layout, it is necessary to consider the following questions that will determine the nature of the layout, for example the maximum space that it can occupy. Remember that you need to leave some access room around the

Seen from above, this OO scale layout is roughly 1.5m square, but in that space there is a large scenic section plus storage sidings to the rear.

layout. Resist the urge to make the layout so big that you cannot get to it.

Will the layout be exhibited at model railway shows? If it is, the baseboards will need to be portable. Can the baseboards be carried in a car, or will a van need to be hired to carry them to shows? If the baseboards are to be portable, can you carry them on your own, or will assistance always be needed? What sort of supports will the layout require?

It is a good idea to make a list of the features that you want to incorporate on the layout before starting to draw up a track plan. These may include, for example, a locomotive depot, a goods yard, a dockside scene, hidden storage and so on. Where is the layout to be modelled upon? Do you have just one favourite prototype line, which may make your choice of a model railway easier? Determine the longest train

Give advance thought to how a layout will be carried. Here, new baseboards are carried in a Vauxhall Vectra, but once the scenery was added the layout became too large to carry in the car and a van had to be hired to transport it to a show.

that will be able to be used on the layout – this will be the length of the storage sidings or loops. Do you want a predominantly scenic layout, or one with lots of tracks, leaving little room for scenery? Will you use DC or DCC control, or a mixture of both?

Will the points be manually operated, or by point motor or cable? The answer to this question may affect the positioning of the points on the layout in relation to access and the baseboard supports. What is to be the widest section of the baseboards? Will all parts of the layout be easily accessible for track clean-ing, derailments and refurbishment of the scenery?

Will you want to use your long-established build-ing techniques, or will you want to experiment with new methods on the new layout? These might include, for example, different baseboard construc-tion, using flexible instead of sectional track, trying out new scenic techniques and so on. If either money or time is in short supply, could the layout be designed so that part of it could be completed and then when resources are forthcoming the next stage could be built? Could the layout be designed so as to be expandable?

Single-unit trains are a great way to add an entire train in a short length. Here a Hornby Class 153 DMU stands next to a converted Lima Class 121 unit. The Class 121 unit is around 30mm (1.2in) shorter than the more modern Class 153 unit. Both of the units depicted are OO scale, but N-scale models of the same units are available from Dapol.

These are just a number of the questions that we may need to ask ourselves when we are about to build a new layout. There are no right or wrong answers – these questions are simply a tool to enable us to build the layout with which we will be most satisfied.

PLANNING THE CURVES

On most model railway layouts it is generally best to use the largest radius curves that your space permits. In reality, the only real railways that feature sharp curves are those in dockyards and at industrial locations such as collieries. Sharp curves will not look too out of place on a model of a narrow-gauge mountain line in Wales, but they will look totally out of place on an LMS mainline or a model of the high-speed standard-gauge line such as High Speed 1.

The radius of a curve is the length of a line from the centre of the curve to its outer edge. Manufacturers retail a range of sectional curves usually including an R in their descriptions. So, for example, an R1 might be the smallest sectional radius curve and R6 might be their largest radius curve. For curves larger than R6, it is usually necessary to use flexible track.

Some manufacturers specify that their locomotives and rolling stock should use a minimum radius of a number of centimetres. Bachmann, for example, specifies that its locomotives should only be used on R2 track (radius 2 track) and above. The instruction leaflet of locomotives or the manufacturers' catalogues are the best places to find the suggested minimum radii.

Use the largest radius curves that your baseboard will allow. Graceful curves on model railways look a lot better than sharp ones. The trains will run better too. Be very careful that any S bends on a layout use curves that are as large a radius as possible. Sharp radius S curves will mean that the train will move unprototypically through the track formation – the carriages will not move gracefully and it will be impossible to maintain close-coupled carriage connections.

Use curves that have the largest radius feasible for your layout. If you are making a tunnel entrance, test it with your longest item of rolling stock before fixing the tunnel mouth to the layout.

CONCLUSION

The aim of this chapter has been to bring various layout planning aids to your attention. Layouts are very personal to the builder and display his choices and preferences.

Two notes of warning are necessary: firstly, sad to say, not all published track plans are either workable or realistic. Some layout designers just try to squeeze too much track on to a baseboard. If you have some doubt as to whether a track plan is workable, use the Peco paper templates or Hornby's plastic quarter-scale pieces before starting to lay the track. Secondly, do not be tempted just to design layouts for the rest of your modelling life. Beware of becoming an 'armchair modeller' – someone who never actually gets round to building the layouts that they have designed!

Sharing track plans and layout proposals with other modellers is a good way to test out a design. There are a number of excellent railway modelling websites from which you can gain views, help and advice from other modellers (see the Appendices).

There are lots of track-planning books available in the UK, mainland Europe and the USA. Track planning is one of the armchair aspects of the hobby that many enjoy tremendously.

Peco's Setrack Planbooks are good value for money at around £3 each and contain tested plans of how to make layouts in N and OO scales quickly. The introductory pages contain much advice on building a layout.

More track planning books that comprehensively discuss the various layout formation possibilities, combined with splendid artwork that encourages one to start a new layout.

Layout Design Essentials

- A solid and level baseboard is essential for good track laying. There is no shortcut to this! You will regret it if you lay track on a poor-quality baseboard.
- Use paper templates from Peco to see which pieces of track you will need. Hornby's quarter-scale plastic track pieces are another useful way of laying out the track plan to see exactly how it will look full size.
- Consider some of the track-planning PC programs to assist you in planning the track layout and experiment with pieces of track on your baseboard before determining the final track plan and fixing the track down.
- Use isolating points (those that do not carry the current to the line once the point is changed) to reduce the number of electrical connections if you wish to keep the wiring simple. Alternatively, by using DCC control you will not need isolating points.
- If you are going to fit point motors, think ahead – where are they going to go? Can they be fitted beneath the baseboard, or do they need to be situated alongside the point?
- As you fix the track down, make sure that the rails and fishplates fit together properly. Push the pieces of sectional track together on a flat surface. Run your finger along the top of the rails as you lay the track to ensure that the joints are all smooth. A misaligned track connection will derail trains.
- If you are a newcomer to the hobby and are tempted to jump immediately to using flexible track, think again. Valuable experience can be learned by using sectional track. If you begin by using sectional track and later decide to change over to flexible track, those sectional pieces can still be used, for example in hidden sidings and storage yards.
- Be relaxed and enjoy designing track plans, but do not enjoy planning too much because you may never actually build a layout!

Figures placed in realistic poses can help a layout come alive. This modern station security personnel figure is from the Bachmann Scenecraft range.

SPACING-SAVING SECTOR PLATE

The Noch three-way segment turntable is a real space-saver. Though they were not often seen on the UK rail network, as something 'a little different' they are a well-made accessory that can be digitally controlled.

The Noch segment turntable takes short locomotives such as Class 03 and 08 diesels, plus Panniers and Jinties. The three-way action reduces the necessary length of a layout by more than 300mm (12in).

A COMPACT LAYOUT

This OO-scale layout was built on a 122 x 30cm (4 x 1ft) baseboard. Four cork carpet tiles were glued to the top of the baseboard to absorb the noise of the trains. Mainly sectional track was used, but the sidings were pieces of flexible track cut to length. The building is an adapted plastic kit by US firm Pikestuff.

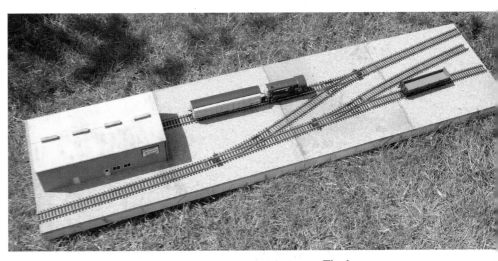

The layout was built to stand on the author's office desk and because a lightweight timber frame was used, the layout could be easily moved around the house. Merkur retaining walls ran along the rear of the layout so that a back scene was not needed. This layout was made in less than two days in the garden in fine weather.

Preiser figures walk around the completed layout. Small details such as these elevate the layout, which is really just a small shunting yard.

STORAGE SIDINGS

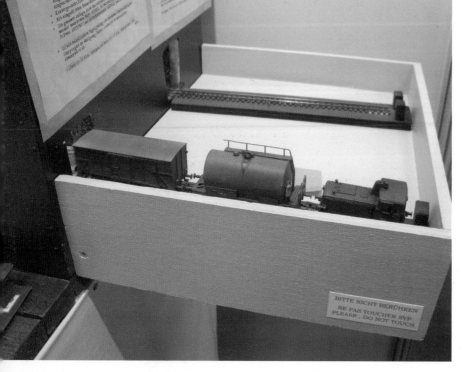

CLOCKWISE FROM TOP LEFT:

Storage sidings can be hidden under the scenery or indeed other tracks. Here Stephan Kraus has installed three storage loops under the main line on his Swiss narrow-gauge model using HOm track. Stephan is a professional layout builder (www.modellbau-smk.de).

This is one alternative for storage sidings using a Y and a left- and a right-hand point. The sidings can either form dead ends or be loops of track.

Short stub-end sidings on this HO-scale layout need 'hand shunting', but because there are no points the length of the storage yard can be kept short. This is not everyone's cup of tea, but it is one modelling possibility for a storage yard.

A SCENIC INTERLUDE

CLOCKWISE FROM TOP LEFT:

Today's ready-to-run locomotives feature separate handrails, sometimes sprung buffers, are ready weathered, DCC Ready or DCC Fitted, or sometimes DCC Sound . Never have railway modellers had it so good!

This end of the platform scene uses resin huts from Hornby Skaledale, plastic accessories such as pallets and oil drums, a Ratio kit-built signal and signs by Tiny Signs.

A Heljan Hymek trundles slowly through a rural scene in the days of the much-missed BR Blue era.

CHAPTER FOUR

CHOOSING THE RIGHT SCALE FOR YOU

Modelling in the right scale for you is an important factor for enjoying the hobby.

Everyone's personal circumstances are different and so what may be the right scale for your model railway may not be right for another modeller. We all have different amounts of space, time, knowledge and money. Some of us may long for a large layout, while others are content with a compact line. The skill when considering the various scales is to choose the one that will give you the most satisfaction.

This superb night-time scene is based on the Busch mining train system. The HO scale system uses a track system of 6.5mm rail gauge and two radii of curves plus straights and points. There is a central magnetic strip that runs centrally between the rails that can be disguised by ballast. BUSCH/GOLDEN VALLEY HOBBIES

HOW TO NARROW DOWN YOUR CHOICE

Around two-thirds of railway modellers in the UK work in OO scale. Both OO and N scales provide very good starting points, because a large number of manufacturers are currently producing all the necessary bits and pieces for each scale. The number of products now being produced in O scale in particular is increasing all the time.

Some modellers find that as they get older the larger scales are more suitable to their eyesight and the flexibility of their hands and fingers. There are some superb O-scale layouts to be seen

An O-scale layout, this time John Emerson's Gifford Street, which displays good quality scenic work. O scale is destined to become much more popular in the near future as various companies begin to make ready-to-run O-scale locomotives at prices not much more expensive than OO-scale DCC-ready locomotives.

Ian Futers is one of the UK's most prolific layout builders. Here is a glimpse of one of his many Scottish essays in O scale, called Victoria Square.

If the space you have for a layout is small, why not try the Busch Feldbahn system, which is HO scale but with Z-scale track. BUSCH/GOLDEN VALLEY HOBBIES

These two Ford Explorer road vehicles are made by US manufacturer Atlas (www.atlasrr. com), highlighting the big size difference between HO and N scales. The N-scale vehicle is effectively a quarter of the size of the HO one.

now at model railway shows and the number of ready-to-run O-scale locomotives, rolling stock and accessories now available from companies including Dapol, Heljan, Ixion and Peco make O scale a much easier modelling proposition compared to just a few years ago.

If the room that you have available for a model railway is small, then N scale may your best option. It might help you to get sweeping curves and trains running 'in the landscape' rather than just trackwork filling up a narrow baseboard in OO and O scales.

If the layout is for a child or a young person, OO scale might be the best because its locomotives and rolling stock are easier for small hands to hold. If you enjoy fine-detailing locomotives and making scenes, then OO might again be the most suitable scale to begin with. The number of available accessories is greater in OO scale than any other scale. OO scale is 1/72 and HO scale is 1/87, but they use the same track. That is why we sometimes see the term OO/HO. UK manufacturers work to OO scale, whilst European and US manufacturers work to HO scale.

Wharfedale Road is an OO-scale compact layout built especially for the Right Track DVD, Layout Planning and Design. It shows what can be achieved by using mainly 'off the peg' products. For more information go to: www.model-railway-dvd.co.uk/ right_track19.php. PAUL MARSHALL-POTTER

This compact layout built by Chris Nevard provides a lot of visual interest, including both industrial buildings and a wharf. CHRIS NEVARD/MODEL RAIL

Z gauge has for a long time been the smallest scale for ready-to-run products, using a scale of 1/220. It enables a layout to be built on a coffee table, a window sill or just a shelf in your bookcase. Märklin manufactures a variety of Z-scale equipment. T Gauge at 1/450 scale is now the smallest model railway scale in the world, with a track gauge of only 3mm. The models are powered by 4.5V DC motors and motor coaches feature magnetic wheels. In the UK it is available from Gaugemaster.

Of course, some modellers like more than one scale and have layouts (or at least dioramas) in each of the scales that are their favourites.

IS N SCALE A GOOD STARTING POINT?

N scale can be a very good starting point in the hobby because of the proactive manufacturer support for the scale. The last few years have seen a huge increase in good-quality products for N scale, including locomotives, rolling stock, buildings

One corner of an N-scale Minitrix demonstration layout seen at the 2014 Nuremberg Toy Fair showing the good scenic potential of the smaller scales.

A finished Woodland Scenics Lightweight Scenic Ridge layout fitted snugly into a Vauxhall Vectra hatchback car. Because the baseboard was made from hard foam, it was moveable in one hand. The Woodland Scenics Lightweight Scenic Ridge Layout Kit (stock number ST1482) contains most of the parts to enable this 0.9 x 1.8m (3 x 6ft) N-scale layout to be built with inclines, hills, valleys, tunnels, bridges, roads and landscaping. The layout accommodates one train providing a run of over 6m (20ft).

and many accessories. If the room that is available for a model railway is small, N scale may be your best option. That way, you can watch trains running 'in the landscape', with long, sweeping curves and proper hillsides.

The scenic skills required on N-scale layouts are somewhat different to those on OO and larger scales. Tall, static grass fibres do not really have a place on N layouts and it is probably best to stick with good-quality fine foam scatter, such as Woodland Scenics Fine Turf, for the main landscaping.

HELPFUL WEBSITES

Here are some websites that might help your decision-making process:
- www.bachmann.co.uk/beginers.php   (a   useful summary of scales).
- www.gauge0guild.com.
- www.2mm.org.uk.
- www.doubleogauge.com.
- www.gaugemaster.com (for Kato N, Märklin Z and T Gauge products).
- www.newrailwaymodellers.co.uk (a useful website for those new to the hobby).

Kato Glacier Express – A Hybrid Train

The Glacier Express is one of the world's most famous trains operating between the Swiss Alpine resorts of St Moritz to Zermatt. The prototype railway network uses 1m narrow-gauge track. To model such a network in HO scale, HOm track is usually used and Nm in N scale (this means 1m-scale track width in HO and N scales). However, Kato has produced a locomotive and coaches to run on N-scale standard-gauge track. So while this is not exactly prototypical, it does open up more modelling possibilities for those wanting to model Swiss narrow-gauge trains on the more readily available N-scale track.

There are two sets that together make up the complete train and incidentally Bemo, the manufacturer of models of Swiss narrow-gauge railways mainly in HOm scale, has announced that it is going to produce models of Swiss narrow-gauge trains to run on standard-gauge HO track.

For more information go to http://www.katomodels. com/product/nmi/glacier_exp_e.shtml. In the UK, Kato products are distributed by Gaugemaster (www.gauge-master.com).

Kato makes N-scale models of the metre-gauge Glacier Express trains to run on standard-gauge N-scale track. Noch and other companies make N-scale preformed layouts such as the one seen here.

Busch Feldbahn System Offers a Lot of Railway in a Small Space

The Feldbahn (field railway) system by Busch offers great potential for narrow-gauge modelling in small spaces. The HO-scale track system consists of 6.5mm rail gauge and two radii of curves, plus straights and points. There is a central magnetic strip that runs between the rails, which can be disguised by ballast. There are several starter sets, plus a number of different wagons.

Busch expands this system year on year with different themes, including a paper mill with a gatehouse, factory, warehouse, paper rolls and cellulose bales, along with a matching narrow-gauge locomotive, wagons and matching vans, trucks and excavators.

For more information, go to www.busch-model.com. In the UK, Busch products are distributed by Golden Valley Hobbies (www.goldenvalleyhobbies.com).

This HO-scale layout is basically an oval of track with a loop and a couple of sidings. It uses 6.5mm track from Busch and the entire scenic layout measures just over 1 x 0.5m (3.3 x 1.6ft).

The Busch Feldbahn system offers a lot of railway in a very small space. This scene features narrow-gauge and standard-gauge railways. *BUSCH/GOLDEN VALLEY HOBBIES*

The Busch Feldbahn system has a brickworks train with a range of suitable buildings and accessories. *BUSCH/ GOLDEN VALLEY HOBBIES*

ADAPTING N-SCALE EQUIPMENT TO REPRESENT A MINIATURE RAILWAY

CLOCKWISE FROM TOP LEFT:

Did you say that you had no room for a layout? Why not use N-scale track to represent a miniature railway? This tiny layout will be made up from four different scenes and measures just 75 x 60cm (30 x 24in).

This is a part of a farmyard scene on the quartet of miniature railway scenes. Loco modifications by Dave Lowery.

This miniature railway uses Graham Farish N-scale rolling stock, but G-scale figures have been added to create the illusion of a miniature railway. Here are the finished four parts comprising of a zoo, a stately home, a farm and a beach scene. This layout was built especially for the Bachmann Times, which is the quarterly magazine of the Bachmann Collectors Club.

SWISS INTERLUDE

Cavalata, a Swiss-based layout, was made by Stephan Kraus. The track is HOm scale with rolling stock by Bemo. STEPHAN KRAUS

Another scene of Stephan Kraus's Cavalata layout.
STEPHAN KRAUS

SCENIC INTERLUDE

Just one distinctive feature of a real location can set the theme for a layout. Here the very narrow road bridge on the Auchmuty branch in Scotland is under construction.

The finished bridge in OO scale. BR Class 08 locomotives really did squeeze that tightly through the bridge!

Timber loading sidings do not take up a lot of room, but can add visual interest to a corner of a layout.

Peco's relay boxes and trunking are good ways to make the lineside more complete on modern image layouts.

These clumps of daffodils were made by adding yellow foam scatter material on to the tops of grass tufts with a little PVA adhesive.

CHAPTER FIVE

HOW TO BUILD BASEBOARDS

Build a good baseboard and you are on the way to making a good layout.

The baseboard is one of the fundamental parts of a layout. Good, well-built baseboards are important in contributing to satisfaction within the hobby. Conversely, warping baseboards that lead to derailments will detract from your enjoyment. If the construction of the baseboards is good, the chances are that the trains will run well and the layout will last a long time.

GENERAL ADVICE

There are many good model railway books and leaflets describing how to make baseboards and these will assist your woodworking skills and knowledge. These include: *Railway Modelling: the Realistic Way* by Iain Rice; the Peco Setrack OO/HO and N scale Planbooks and the *Peco Shows You How* booklet on building baseboards.

Read layout construction articles in model railway magazines to see what tips you can pick up from other modellers. When visiting model railway shows, look at the baseboard construction of the layouts. Most exhibitors are particularly proud of their baseboards and the supporting legs. Chat with the operators and they will be ready to pass on the lessons they learned. Various layout-building firms attend the largest model railway shows and it is worth chatting to their representatives and looking at their products. Even if you do not order a layout from them, you will be able to gain ideas and see the latest construction techniques.

Enjoy building the baseboards. It is best to view them as more than just a necessary part of the layout-building process. Though most of the baseboard will not be seen by the viewing public, the better the baseboard construction, the better the layout will be.

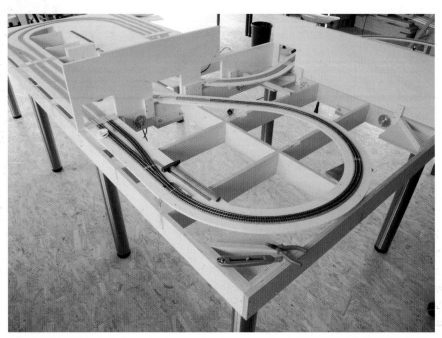

An open-plan baseboard built by SMK Modellbau of Germany, which specializes in making layouts for customers anywhere in Europe.
STEPHAN KRAUS

MAKING BASEBOARDS FROM TIMBER

We do not need to have an A Level in carpentry to build robust baseboards, because it is a skill that can be learned. The criteria that you are aiming for with each baseboard is lightness yet strength, a smooth top surface and something that will accept pins, such as those that hold the track on to the baseboard.

As you plan to build the baseboards, consider their size and weight. The bigger the baseboard, the more difficult it will be to carry and to store. The heavier the baseboard, the more difficult it will be to move, especially if you are working on your own. Baseboards measuring 1.2 x 0.6m (4 x 2ft) are generally accepted to be the maximum size that is suitable for regular movement by one person.

If you do feel nervous about building a baseboard, begin by making a diorama baseboard. This will give you the confidence to tackle larger baseboards later. Building a diorama baseboard will provide experience of measuring the timber, cutting out the baseboard surface, making the framework and attaching all the component parts together using a variety of techniques, including glue, nails and screws. For the various fittings that will assist baseboard construction, go to: www.stationroadbaseboards.co.uk/menu_fittings.htm

A top surface of a baseboard can use plywood, MDF, Sundeala or other timber sheets. These can be cut to size at some local DIY stores or timber merchants. Use planed timber for the framework of the baseboard. Again this can be cut to length at your DIY store or timber merchant. Though this is more expensive than rougher timber it will look a lot nicer and is far less hazardous to your fingers as you move it and work with it. Planed timber will certainly make the final layout look a lot more professional. Timber measuring 50 x 25mm (2 x 1in) is generally suitable for this purpose.

Think how to get the baseboard top and framework parts home from the DIY store. Will it fit in your car? Do you know someone with a large van who might be able to move it for you?

As you assemble the baseboard, use adhesive in addition to screws and nails to fix the timber frame-

A two-baseboard layout showing the three sets of legs shared between the two baseboards. The top surface is plywood, with the frame being made from 2 x 1 planed timber.

The same baseboard and supporting legs in its upright position just waiting for the layout to be built.

This close-up of a corner of the baseboard shows the three-ply top and the frame of planed timber. The pieces of the frame have been screwed together as the top has been fixed to the frame. The holes have been countersunk so that the screws do not protrude above the surface of the baseboard.

The legs have been fixed to the baseboard using long threaded bolts and wing nuts, which provide a good way of offering a quick and easy release when assembling and disassembling the layout. A washer has been used between the timber leg and the wing nut to preserve the condition of the timber.

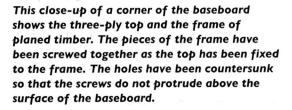

Holes cut out in the supporting timbers before assembly of the baseboard are a good way to carry cables tidily along the length of a layout.

It is always worth marking up the legs and baseboard tops so that an error will not be made when erecting a layout.

work to the baseboard. This is especially so if you intend to move the baseboard around a lot, such as on a portable exhibition layout. The glue will provide secondary rigidity to the baseboard and normal PVA adhesive can be used for this.

Not all of us are naturally good carpenters. If you feel that no matter how hard you try, your baseboards are liable to be poor, consider engaging one of the specialist baseboard-making companies such as Elite Baseboards.

TOOLS

To build a timber baseboard, the toolkit would consist of:

- A pencil – for marking the cuts on the timber.
- An expanding ruler – for marking up the timber and baseboard top.
- A set square – for getting the corners of the baseboard at right angles.
- A plain-saw – for cutting the framework timber and the baseboard top (though a DIY store or timber merchant might do this for you).
- An electric drill (cordless or mains) and selection of drill bits – for drilling the holes in the timber frame and baseboard to countersink screws.
- A screwdriver (manual or electric) – for assembling the frame.
- A selection of screws for fixing the baseboard top to the framework.
- A standard woodworking hammer – for fixing panel pins into the baseboard.
- Panel pins for additional strength between the screws on the baseboard top.
- A 13mm (½in) paintbrush to spread PVA glue on the framework as it is fixed to the baseboard and for attaching the pieces of the framework together.
- A surform – for tidying up the edges of the cut timber.
- Wet & dry paper – for smoothing down the cut edges of the baseboard and frame.

Various different timbers have been used in this layout, including plywood, MDF and planed timber. This layout was built by Model Railway Constructor.

Remember to tidy the look of the edge of your baseboard using something as readily obtainable as a Matt Emulsion Match Pot from a DIY store.

MAKING BASEBOARDS FROM HARD FOAM

Using hard foam for a baseboard will result in a lightweight baseboard when supported by a light timber base. The Woodland Scenics SubTerrain Layout System has an extensive range of pieces that are manufactured from polystyrene, including raised trackbed pieces that are flexible, flat boards, profile boards for around the sides of a layout and incline pieces for taking the track to a different level. These components are light in weight and can be used to fit specific height and incline requirements.

Home roof-insulation foam pieces available from DIY stores sold under various brand names such as Knauf and Celotex are excellent for landscape modelling. Additional pieces of hard foam for the scenery foundations can be found as the packaging around Bachmann Scenecraft and Hornby Skaledale buildings and any domestic white goods. Hard foam sections can easily be cut easily using the Woodland Scenics Hot Wire Foam Cutter or its Foam Knife (with its long blades) with very little mess. I find Woodland Scenics Foam Tack Glue to be quicker

A piece of the Woodland Scenics SubTerrain hard foam with a very useful long-bladed Foam Knife, made by the same company.

Hard foam pieces by Woodland Scenics have been used on a timber frame. These corner profile boards have been cut and the glue is setting as the pieces are held in position with Foam Nails.

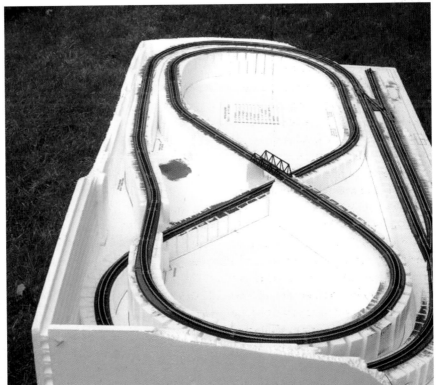

This N-scale layout measures 1.8 x 0.9m (6 x 3ft) and is made from Woodland Scenics SubTerrain pieces on a timber-base frame.

drying than PVA adhesive. Whilst the glue is drying, use Woodland Scenics Foam Nails (T-pins) to hold the pieces firmly together.

For added strength, gluing pieces of mounting cardboard to the underside of the foam is a cheap and simple way of increasing the rigidity of the baseboard while adding little extra weight to it. The resultant baseboards are very light, even after the addition of the plaster cloth, the track and the buildings. While a hard foam baseboard would not stand up to a huge amount of moving and it is more fragile than a timber-frame baseboard, there are good possibilities for using hard foam on layouts. If a framework of timber was made and the foam sheets attached to that, the resultant baseboard would be strong, yet lightweight.

For more information about the Woodland Scenics SubTerrain range, go to www.woodlandscenics.com. In the UK, Woodland Scenics products are distributed by Bachmann. The company's website (www.bachmann. co.uk) lists the products (with prices), together with a list of UK dealers stocking these products. For additional information, it might be useful to get a copy of the *SubTerrain Manual* (ST1402) and the DVD *SubTerrain: Build a Layout Fast and Easy* (DVD-ST1400).

TOOLS

• To go with its SubTerrain System, Woodland Scenics produces a range of dedicated tools and adhesives specifically for working with hard foam. These tools are useful for other scenic modelling techniques; for example, Foam Nails are a useful tool whatever materials you are working with. These T-pins are sold in packs of seventy-five and are 5mm (2in) long and are good for holding together hard foam pieces or other materials whilst the glue sets.

• A Foam Knife (with some spare blades) is good for cutting through the thick pieces of foam. Its blades are longer than average blades for cutting through

blocks of hard foam up to 5mm (2in) thick. Foam Tack Glue fixes the hard foam pieces together. It comes ready mixed in a 12fl oz plastic bottle. This is useful for working with all polystyrene and also as a modelling 'filler'. Hard foam can be cut easily and quickly using the Woodland Scenics Hot Wire Foam Cutter.

• A surform is a good way to smooth any pieces of hard foam. A steel ruler is useful for cutting straight edges in the foam, while a vacuum cleaner is handy for sucking up any leftover bits.

GETTING BASEBOARDS MADE FOR YOU

If you feel that no matter how long you practise using a saw, your baseboards are still liable to be poor, consider employing one of the specialist baseboard-making companies, which include:

• B & R Model Railways, offering custom-built baseboards that can be ordered online at www.bandrmodelrailways.co.uk.

• Elite Baseboards (www.elitebaseboards.net), offering modular baseboards, bespoke baseboards, plus a layout planning service, CAD design, tracklaying and wiring for DCC or DC.

• Model Baseboard Manufacturers, supplying kits for the Hornby Trakmat and other sizes (www.modelshopuk.com).

• Model Railway Solutions (www.modelrailwaysolutions.co.uk), offering baseboard-building services, helix, baseboard accessories and more.

• White Rose (www.whiterosemodelworks.co.uk), selling a plug and latch system that makes erecting the baseboards quick and easy. The company's bespoke board service includes laying track to your plans, plus complete electrics.

This professionally built baseboard by Elite Baseboards uses plywood with holes cut out of the supporting timbers to reduce the weight.

The holes to take the screws are well hidden on this baseboard made by Elite Baseboards.

Nine-ply wood was used on this lightweight baseboard built by Elite Baseboards with screws well out of harm's way in sunken holes.

CHAPTER SIX

FORMING THE LANDSCAPE

Landscape turns bare baseboards into a model railway.

Just how do we set about making the landscape when starting with a flat baseboard or open framework layout? There are a great variety of methods using all sorts of different materials. We will outline several of the alternatives here for you to choose which method you want to adopt.

MAKING THE CONTOURS OF THE LAND

The trackbed needs good, firm support on any layout. Ideally, it will not just look like the track has been positioned on top of a flat baseboard, but rather that the track is situated in the landscape as it would be in reality. Once the size of the layout has been determined, consideration can be given to the construction of the baseboard and the landscape.

Land contours form the rear and side perimeters of any layout. In addition, the slope of the land is formed by any intermediate land contours. Land contours can be made from: timber, including hardboard, plywood, Sundeala board or MDF; thick cardboard, such as mounting card; foam board; roof-insulation hard foam material; any of the proprietary layout-building materials, such as the Woodland Scenics SubTerrain System or the Noch Terra-Form System.

When using timber or card for the land contours, it is necessary to use intermediate supporting formers at approx 15cm (6in) intervals. The contour sections can be fixed to the baseboard with PVA adhesive, or by using a hot glue gun. Tape can be used to hold the upright land contours in place whilst the PVA glue dries – joints fixed with hot glue may need no support except from your hand for a few seconds.

This scene is just 30cm (12in) back to front. The steel bridge was made from a Kibri plastic kit, the hard foam supports and rocks are by Noch, with foliage from a number of companies including Heki and Woodland Scenics.

Quarrying hard foam in 4mm; hard foam is a very versatile material for modelling the landscape. It is easy to cut, light in weight, takes tree trunks well and is not that messy to work with.

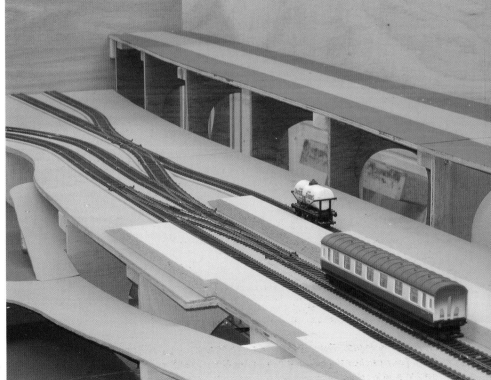

This baseboard demonstrates the levels that make a layout look both realistic and visually interesting. The grey painted sections are to be roads. This layout was built by Bill Carmen.

RAISING THE TRACKBED ABOVE THE BASEBOARD

There are various methods for raising the track above a level baseboard. These include: dropping certain sections of the baseboard so as to create a valley, with the higher trackbed then running on a bridge, viaduct or embankment; raising the trackbed on pieces of roof-insulation hard foam, which can be done for the entire layout with embankments then cut into the hard foam; using a plywood base and raising the trackbed on timber blocks; and using the Woodland Scenics SubTerrain range of hard foam and incline pieces to create a raised trackbed.

SCENERY FOUNDATIONS FOR THE LAYOUT

The materials that are suitable for scenery foundations depend upon the scale of the landscape. Simply, the bigger the scenery, the stronger the support for the scenery will need to be. Is the layout to be portable, or permanent? If the layout is to be portable, it needs to be both strong but also light in weight. One alternative for portable layouts where the scenery is likely to be heavy is to use detachable sections of hills, villages and so on – care will, of course, need to be taken to ensure that the join between the baseboard and the detachable scenery is as seamless as possible.

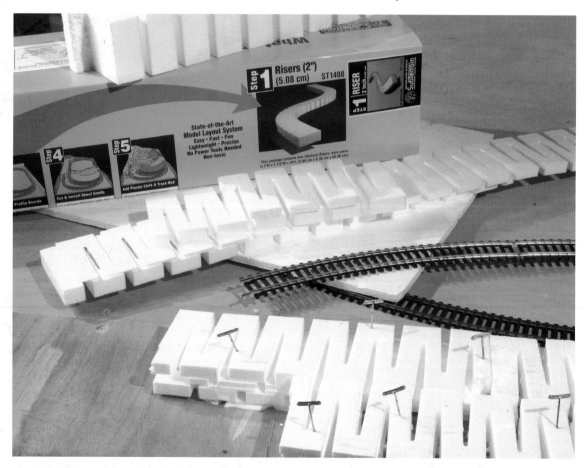

The Woodland Scenics SubTerrain system has various component parts, including a number of different shaped hard foam (polystyrene) pieces that work in conjunction with each other to become landscape formers, raised support for the track. Pre-cut track inclines with 2 per cent, 3 per cent or 4 per cent gradients and a whole range of accessories and tools make the task easy and quick. The resulting layout is lightweight.

If the landscape is to be covered in trees, buildings, rock faces and the like, it is likely to become quite heavy. Scenery that is just foliage or grass will be a lot lighter in weight. The more weight that will need to be supported, the stronger the land contours and scenery foundations will need to be. Do you need detachable sections of scenery to provide access to tunnels and storage yards? If so, these sections will need to be carefully made so as not to leave an obvious gap around the joins.

On this layout the front baseboard was stepped down from the baseboard at the back. This provided the possibility of making a long, sweeping embankment at the front of the layout.

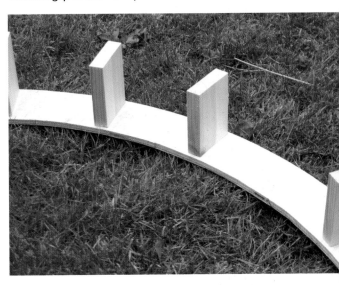

The timber sub-baseboard for the curved section of track was made from plywood, with the supporting timbers being planed timber.

Cutting to size the timber sub-baseboard for the curved section of track using a small saw.

A test run on the top of the embankment was carried out on unballasted track on the curved sub-baseboard.

Gaugemaster foam ballast was used on this layout, which, once bedded into the adjacent landscape and the track weathered, looked jolly good and kept the noise of the passing trains to a minimum.

This is the same location after the scenic work had been completed.

HOW TO FILL THE SPACE BETWEEN THE LAYOUT CONTOURS

Once the landscape formers have been shaped and fixed to the baseboards, attention needs to be given as to how to fill in the space between the land contours. There is a variety of alternatives that include: crumpled newspaper or parcel packing paper pushed between the contour formers and then covered with plaster-impregnated cloth; a web of strips of cardboard fixed to the landscape formers and to each other using hot glue, PVA adhesive or a staple gun; and chicken wire spread between, and fixed to, the top of the contour formers. Another option is to drape masking tape across the top of the formers to form a matrix. Domestic masking tape normally used for decorating is suitable for this. The closer together the tape, the stronger the web will be to take plaster-impregnated cloth.

Brown parcel packing paper has been used between the SubTerrain components to form the basis of the land. The brown paper will be covered with plaster cloth.

A simple web of strips of cardboard can be fixed to the landscape formers and to each other using hot glue, PVA adhesive or a staple gun. This will support the plaster cloth to be laid over the top.

Noch produces landscape foundation parts called the Terra-Form System, which uses timber dowel posts and fixing plugs to produce a lightweight basis for hills, embankments or similar. Woodland Scenics Ready Landforms are plastic-based shapes already covered with scatter material. These landforms are sold in a number of sizes and shapes.

A light steel mesh that can be bought from a car repair shop or sold as a model railway product by Busch, Noch or other firms can also be used. This will usually require a timber frame to which to attach the wire. Heavy duty crêpe paper is also available from Noch or an art shop. This can be fixed to the formers with a staple gun or hot glue. Busch produces a dedicated landscape system that incorporates heavy duty crêpe paper.

LEFT: *Ready ballasted RocoLine track sits on top of planed timber offcuts, bolstered to the correct height by additional pieces of thick cardboard. This will be an embankment that will be supported by the cardboard contour formers to be fixed to the baseboard with hot glue.*

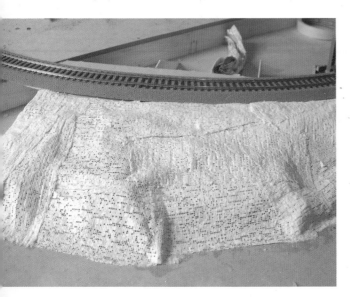

RIGHT: *Newspaper was laid between the cardboard contour formers. Plaster cloth will be added over the top of the formers and newspaper.*

LEFT: *Plaster cloth after it has been spread over the top of the newspaper. It will now need to be painted, then treated scenically.*

RAISING THE TRACKBED WITH WOODLAND SCENICS SUBTERRAIN

The Woodland Scenics SubTerrain System offers a comprehensive landscaping system with dedicated adhesives, tools, instruction books and DVDs. It has various component parts including a number of different shaped hard foam (polystyrene) pieces that work in conjunction with each other to form landscape formers, raised support for the track, pre-cut track inclines with 2 per cent, 3 per cent or 4 per cent gradients and a whole range of accessories and tools to make the task easy, lightweight, quick and not very messy.

Because the Woodland Scenics SubTerrain System components are made from hard foam they are light in weight and are thus ideally suited for use on a portable layout. This is especially useful if a layout is to be taken to shows. To go along with the SubTerrain System, Woodland Scenics produces a range of dedicated tools and adhesives that are also useful for other scenic modelling techniques and methods.

Hard foam is very easy to cut with a sharp knife and is lightweight, which is ideal for portable layouts. A Woodland Scenics Foam Knife will cut through foam of up to 5mm (2in) thickness.

PVA adhesive works well with hard foam, but Foam Tack Glue dries more quickly.

How to Use Plaster Cloth

One of the most often used materials in scenery making is plaster-impregnated cloth. It usually comes as a white cloth in rolls and is available at many model shops under the names of Mod-Roc, Peco Landform and Woodland Scenics Plaster Cloth.

It is simple and quick to use at most angles of landscape. Firstly, the cloth needs to be cut, using scissors, into pieces of approximately 100sq cm (15.5sq in). Then hang the pieces individually in water in a mixing bowl (used only for scenery making) for a few seconds until the piece is completely wet. Hold the piece at each corner so that it stays 'open' and does not roll up. Remove the piece from the water after a few seconds and wipe the edge of the cloth on the lip of the bowl as you remove it to get rid of any excess water.

Lay the pieces of plaster cloth over the edge of the contour formers and padding material and take a little time to remove any creases or ripples with your fingers. The cloth will stay workable for a few minutes. Lay all the pieces so that they overlap each other. The better quality cloths do not always require two layers; they may be rigid enough with just one.

Once the cloth is dry, the entire surface will need to be painted so that the white plaster does not show through the subsequent layers of scenic materials. I generally use cheap paints in green, grey, black or brown. Acrylics, poster colours and household water-based emulsion paints are all suitable, or it can be the ideal way to use up those unwanted match pots that you might have in your shed. When the cloth has been painted, leave it until the next day before going to the next stage, when it can be coated with PVA adhesive and covered with scatter materials or static grass.

During 2014, Woodland Scenics introduced over fifty new products, including a Plaster Cloth Modelling Tray, which is ideal for wetting cut pieces of plaster cloth or when making waterfalls, because its silicone base is non-stick. The tray works so much better than a bucket, because the plaster does not stick to the tray and it takes only a couple of minutes to clean up after use.

The Woodland Scenics Plaster Cloth Modelling Tray, which is ideal for wetting cut pieces of plaster cloth, or when making waterfalls. Its silicone base means that plaster does not stick to the surface and it takes only a couple of minutes to clean up after use.

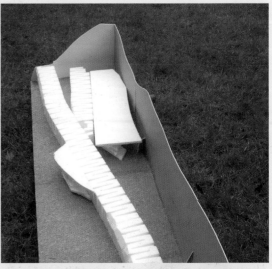

A diorama using hard foam SubTerrain sections to raise the level of the track above the baseboard. Around the edge of the baseboard, mounting card has been used to form the contours of the landscape.

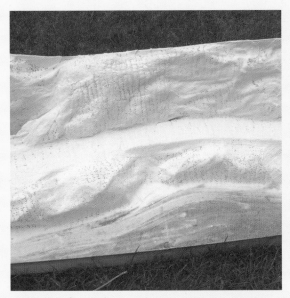

Crumpled newspaper was laid next to the SubTerrain pieces and then covered in plaster cloth that now needs to be painted.

The white plaster cloth was painted with black acrylic paint after the plaster cloth had fully dried and is now ready to be treated scenically.

The final result is a single track line that runs higher than a lake and is backed by a steep embankment.

This simple scene looks so much more interesting because of the different heights of the land. Front to back the baseboard measures just 27cm (11in).

Noch produces landscape foundation parts called the Terra-Form System, which uses timber dowel posts and fixing plugs to produce a lightweight basis for hills, embankments or similar.

Coloured Glue Saves Time

One shortcut to having to paint the land in your scenery is to use glue that is already coloured. You can then apply the scenic materials directly into the glue rather than needing to paint the landscape then brush on adhesive. Busch, Faller, Heki and WW Scenics retail a selection of coloured glues. Alternatively, you can just add brown or green acrylic paint to PVA adhesive to make our own ready-coloured glue. It is best to experiment first with a small amount of your chosen paint to ensure that it mixes well with the PVA adhesive.

For more information about these products, please see the Woodland Scenics catalogue or go to www.woodlandscenics.com. In the UK, Woodland Scenics products are distributed by Bachmann, whose website (www.bachmann.co.uk) lists the products (with prices), together with a list of UK stockists.

USING THE NOCH TERRA-FORM LANDSCAPE SYSTEM

This scenery-building system enables a lightweight base for the land to be made. It is suitable for all scales. Terra-Form System set (stock number 61601) is the basic set and has 228 parts, consisting of wooden dowels, clip-together units, stands, plates and crêpe paper. Once you have mastered the technique of assembling the various component parts, the foundations for scenery can be made quite quickly.

To experiment with the system, try one of the starter sets known as a test pack (stock number 61605) that retails at just over £10.

ADDING A BRIDGE

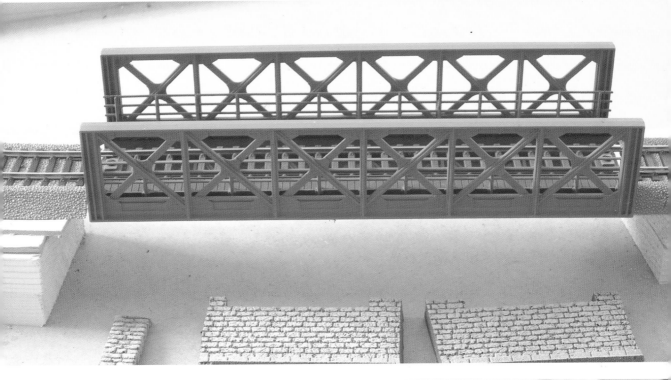

This bridge was made from a simple four-part plastic kit by Roco. The retaining and supporting walls were made from Noch hard foam walling, which is light and very easy to cut and work with.

Bachmann Freightliner Class 66 locomotive crosses the bridge after the scenics were completed around the bridge.

A GLIMPSE OF BOSCARNE JUNCTION

Boscarne Junction is a famous Cornish byway. Fortunately, the station is still open today, forming a terminus on the Bodmin and Wenford Railway. Here is a glimpse of a model interpretation of it built for Model Rail magazine. CHRIS NEVARD/MODEL RAIL

Just some of the tools and materials used whilst making the scenery on one corner of the Boscarne Junction layout.

Spring time at Boscarne. The signal box is a limited edition model by the Kernow Model Centre.

Heljan Railbus leaves the low station platform at Boscarne to run through the lush Cornish countryside.

CHAPTER SEVEN

THE PERMANENT WAY

Good tracklaying contributes to the realism of a layout and to the enjoyment of running trains.

All model railway layouts and dioramas need track. Good tracklaying contributes to the enjoyment of a layout. Bad tracklaying will not inspire onlookers and will leave the modeller wondering if they have chosen the right hobby.

CHOOSING THE RIGHT TRACK FOR YOU

Track for model railways falls, in general terms, into three categories:

• Ready-to-run track sold in sections or pieces and usually referred to as 'sectional track'. These pieces include straight sections, curved sections, crossings and points. This is sometimes also known as 'train

set track', but this does not mean that realistic layouts cannot be made from it.
• Flexible track plus its related components, such as points. This can be used with sectional-track pieces.
• Handmade track that uses a variety of relatively specialist components, including real wood miniature sleepers.

When thinking about what track system to purchase, you should take into account the following considerations. Do you want to lay track quickly and simply? If using sectional track, do you want a system that can be purchased from most towns in the UK, in which case Peco track might be the system for you. What geometry

Real track at Dawlish Warren on the South Devon line. Note the tidy ballasting and point work.

There is plenty of choice of track types available from a number of manufacturers in the most common scales. Here are a few types for OO scale.

suits your room limitations? If your room is compact, sectional curves may be needed. Do you enjoy ballasting, or would you prefer to buy track ready ballasted?

The three basic sectional-track systems (Bachmann, Hornby and Peco) are the cheapest available track and are quite readily available in model shops. Ready-ballasted track is more expensive than non-ballasted track and is not so easy to obtain in the UK.

General advice is that sectional track is a good way forward for beginners and flexible track is for more experienced modellers. Even when one moves 'up' to flexible and/or finescale track, the sectional track that has been bought can be used in the storage yards.

SECTIONAL TRACK

Most of the big-name manufacturers, including Bachmann, Graham Farish and Hornby, retail their own sectional-track systems. Some of their train sets contain track – this is usually an oval of track, with or without a siding. The track supplied with train sets can be expanded by track packs (a specific number of pieces that might, for example, add a loop or a siding to the train set), or by adding any number of additional track pieces from the manufacturers' ranges. Sectional track is well built and robust.

Peco is well known for its ever-expanding ranges of track in various scales. Its OO/HO Setrack is a Universal Code 100 track system with wooden sleepers and nickel silver rail. Various straights, curved points and crossovers are retailed. Peco also sells boxed Setrack Starter Track Sets in N and OO/HO scales. Peco OO-scale Setrack can be combined with its Code 100 flexible track.

Most sectional-track pieces come complete with fitted rail joiners (fishplates), so this is certainly a quick way to start laying track. Sectional-track ranges include such accessories as level crossings, inspection pits, buffer stops, uncoupling units, power connecting clips, track pins and foam ballast inlays for plain track and points.

It is generally quite easy to use sectional pieces of track from different manufacturers interchangeably. If the geometry of the layout does not permit a specific layout, bespoke pieces can be formed by cutting pieces of either sectional or flexible track to fit. To cut track, it is necessary to use a sharp fine-toothed saw, or a pair of rail cutters such as those manufactured by Xuron.

Most sectional-track pieces come with small prepared holes in the sleepers for fixing to the baseboard. Track pins can then be used to fix the track to the baseboard. Use a hollow punch and a small hammer for the initial blow, then take over with the small hammer. If using foam underlay, do not push the track pins too far down, otherwise it will distort the rails and will affect the running of the trains.

In addition to the familiar ready-to-run track systems mentioned above, there are many other track manufacturers from Europe and the USA offering a comprehensive range of track parts. These include:

• Fleischmann, the German manufacturer, produces the Profi range of ready-ballasted track. It is availa-

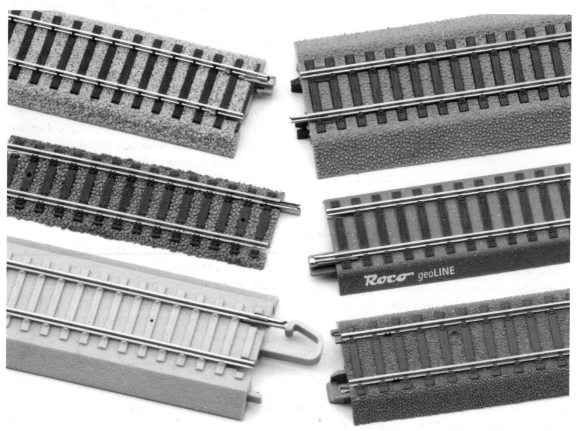

For those who do not want to ballast their track, they can choose ready-ballasted track by Bachmann USA, Fleischmann, Kato, Piko and Roco (GeoLine and RocoLine).

ble in both HO and N scales with the point motors fixed along the side of the turnouts, alleviating the need to make holes in the baseboard. The points are sold in 'live' mode, but the simple removal of wire clips between the tracks converts them into isolating mode.

- Roco produces ready-ballasted HO GeoLine Code 83 track that conceals the point motors in the grey ballast base. Sectional and flexible track is available with a choice of points and crossings.
- The HO range of Märklin uses a third-rail track system. Locomotives pick up the electrical current from small stud contacts located in the centre of the sleepers.
- Kato's Unitrack system for N and OO/HO scales offers track pre-mounted on a plastic base representing the ballast shoulder. Hartel retails track for trams.
- Narrow-gauge modellers are increasingly well catered for by manufacturers. For example, metre-gauge track for HO scale (known as HOm) is available from Bemo, Shinohara and Peco. The Peco 12mm HOm track range includes flexible track, straight and curved points, crossings, buffers and turntables.

FLEXIBLE TRACK

Those who are setting out on a first layout may prefer the simplicity of using sectional track, but if it is realism that you want, finer-scale flexible track is the preferred way forward. Flexible track can be mixed with sectional track where the track is of the same Code (the height of the rail).

The Peco Code 100 flexible-track system is known as the Universal range. Insulated points (Insulfrog) include: catch points; small- and large-radius Y points; small-, medium- and large-radius points for left- and right-hand operation; a three-way medium point; and curved double-radius points. The live frog points (Electrofrog) include: small- and large-radius Y points; small-, medium-and large-radius points for left- and right-hand operation; a three-way medium point; and curved double-radius points.

The Peco Code 75 ('finescale') flexible-track system has live frog points (Electrofrog) with a similar range to the Code 100 insulated range of points. Most of the rolling stock from the current Bachmann, Dapol, Heljan and Hornby OO-scale ranges should run on Code 75 track without any problems due to the fact that wheel flanges are much finer than they were in the past. If you do have any older items of rolling stock that you wish to run on Code 75 track, it is generally quite a simple task to re-wheel the item of stock using modern metal axles from Bachmann or Hornby, or by using finescale replacements from companies including Alan Gibson. There is a Peco product (SL-112) called Combined Rail Joiners, which joins the company's Code 75 and Code 100 rails.

Live frog points may offer better current collection for locomotives, but in my recent experience with modern locomotives I find that they run superbly over insulated points because of multiple wheel current collection. It should be mentioned that live frog points do require more wiring than insulated ones and are probably not worthwhile for a beginner.

Peco also retails a Code 83 line for modellers of North American model railroads. The German company, Tillig, has developed its HO Elite track system with a height profile of 2.07mm with Code 83 rails. The range has a good variety of geometry options. Visually, it is fine profile and has such features as ready-aged rails and one-piece machined-point blades.

Kit-built finer-scale track is available from C&L Finescale (www.finescale.org.uk), Marcway and 'SMP' Scale Model Productions (http://www.marcway.net/smp.php). If you do not feel confident about building your own trackwork, there are various specialists who advertise a track-building service in model railway magazines.

TRACKLAYING – A FEW THOUGHTS

Some followers of our hobby sadly never build a layout because they are daunted by the task of laying track. Tracklaying is not difficult as long as one follows

Laying track with the help of Peco paper templates is a good way of confirming that your track plan does indeed fit on the baseboard and looks good before you purchase the track.

the few basic rules. Using sectional track to begin with will give you confidence in tracklaying because each piece just needs to be pushed together. Track that comes with a train set can be used with the additional pieces that you buy. For example, in OO scale Bachmann, Hornby and Peco Code 100 track is all interchangeable.

Experiment with pieces of track on your baseboard before fixing the track down, or finalizing the track layout. You may discover that a track plan sketched out on paper does not work in reality. It is better to find this out before any track is fixed to the baseboard.

Use Peco paper templates of points and crossings to see how the track layout will look before you buy the wrong pieces of track. These templates can be downloaded and printed at home from www. peco-uk.com and are available for OO and N scales.

Use the largest-radius curves that your baseboard will allow. Sharp curves look especially unrealistic if

you use long bogie wagons and carriages. Do not use S bends unless it is absolutely necessary; they do not look realistic unless they are very sweeping. When using flexible track, a Tracksetta aluminum template is a worthwhile purchase to ensure that curves are laid smoothly.

Special fishplates called isolating fishplates are made from plastic. Once wired, isolated sections of track are useful in locomotive sheds and depots and also in stations. They can be 'switched' to be dead (that is, no power gets through to the rails), so that a locomotive may stand in the section without moving off. With the arrival of DCC, isolated sections of track are not required if all locomotives are fitted with a decoder. Make sure that the rails and the fishplates fit together properly. A misaligned fishplate will derail trains. Push the pieces of track together on a flat surface and run your fingers over all the joints before fixing the track down. Even better, try a test train around the layout before the track is firmly fixed down.

Always use the correct fishplates for the track you have. Here are three different types of Peco fishplates for its OO/HO-scale track systems. One fits Code 75 rails, another Code 83 and the other Code 100.

Where the layout extends along a number of baseboards, the last few centimetres of the track on each baseboard can be soldered to copper-clad sleepers to ensure that the track does not move as the baseboards are separated.

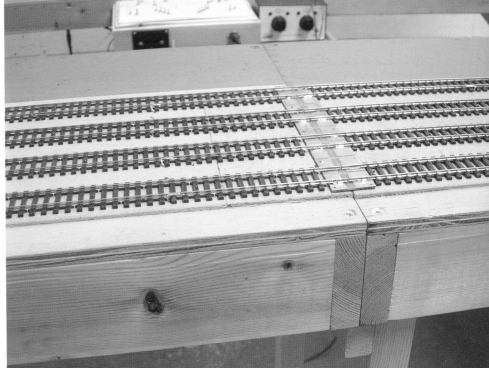

TRACKLAYING DEMONSTRATION

To cut track, use a pair of Xuron track cutters. They cut cleanly and are readily available from model railway shops.

Flexible-track pieces come with rail chairs on all the sleepers, as can be seen in this close-up picture of Code 100 flexible track.

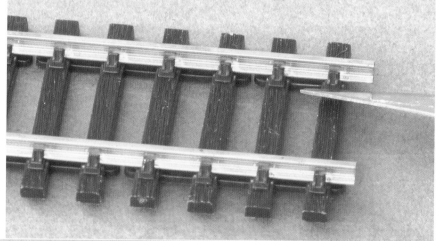

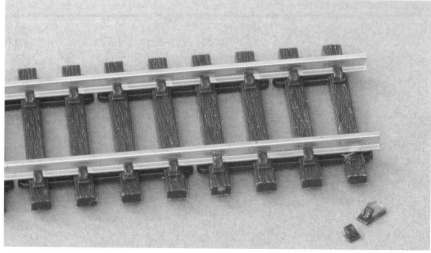

The rail chairs on the last sleeper need to be cut off with a sharp craft knife to give the fishplates sufficient room to fit under and alongside the rail.

Here, the rail chairs on the rail nearest to the camera have been cut off and there is now sufficient space for a fishplate to slide on.

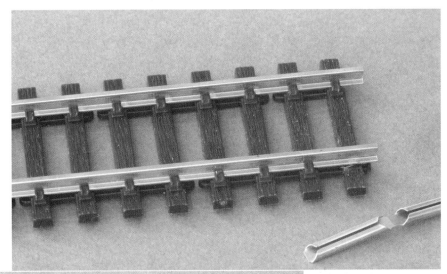

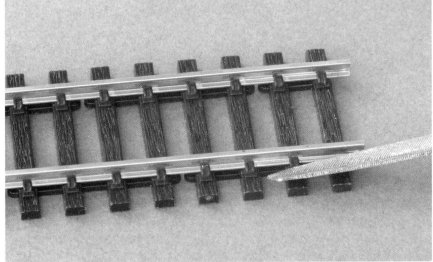

After the rails have been cut to the correct length, they will need filing to remove any sharp edges. Fishplates will not slide on easily if the rails have jagged edges.

It is very important to slide track together on a flat surface to ensure that the fishplates engage correctly with the rails. Always run your finger along the top of the rails to check that the rails are smooth and no joins are misaligned.

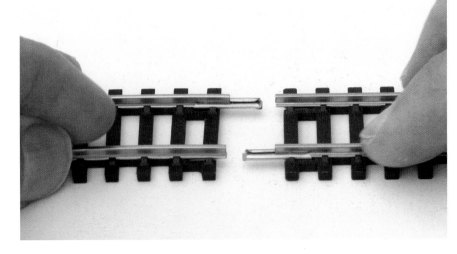

Manufacturers specify that their locomotives and rolling stock should use a minimum radius of a number of centimetres. For example, Bachmann says that its OO-scale locomotives should not use curves less than radius 2. The instruction leaflet of each locomotive or the catalogue will advise on the suggested minimum radius for any particular locomotive.

It is not always necessary to use point motors on a layout if the points are all within easy reach, or if you do not like the idea of wiring the point motors. Use underboard point motors if possible. Point motors located on top of the baseboard do not look prototypical unless they are well hidden. Buy one of the track-cleaning rubber pads (from Peco or Squires, for example) to keep the rails clean. To keep your locomotives in good working order it is best to vacuum off the residual dirt once the rails have been cleaned.

Your trackwork can only ever be as good as your baseboard. A good baseboard pays dividends in terms of the smooth running of your trains. Ensure that all your trackwork is accessible for cleaning. Can it all be reached to replace derailed wagons? Finally, enjoy laying the trackwork – it can be a lot of fun and is a very satisfying task.

TOOLS

Tools needed for tracklaying consist of:

• A craft knife for cutting cork underlay, ballast underlays and to trim the rail chairs off the sleepers when joining flexible track.

Track Terminology

Code 100 This refers to the size of the rail. Code 100 means that the rail height is 100-thousandths of an inch. Code 100 is universal and is used by most popular manufacturers, including Bachmann, Hornby and Peco in OO scale. Code 75 is Peco's finescale track, because the height of the rail is 75-thousandths of an inch.

Fishplates or rail joiners The shaped pieces of thin metal that make the connections between pieces of rail at the end of each piece of track. They conduct the electricity through the rails and come ready installed on sectional track, but need to be added on flexible track. They are sold to fit the rail sizes. Some are made from plastic so that they do not conduct current when used, for example, in sidings.

Flexible track Flexible lengths of track that can be shaped to form gentle curves, sharp curves or simply short or long straights. They are available in all the common scales, with various sleeper types such as concrete or timber.

Frog Part of the point that forms the junction between the two sets of running rails. Some are known as live frogs, where the pieces of rail carry the current, but others are dead frogs with plastic inserts that do not carry the current.

Loop A section of track that is linked by a point at each end. The track in-between is usually parallel to the main line. A train can be stored in a loop while a train passes on the other line.

Point The railway equivalent of a junction, allowing a train to change track, or enter a siding or a loop. Most are two-way, but some are three-way.

Point motors Electric motors that are attached to a point and allow you to change the direction of the point at the touch of a button or switch. They may be attached directly on to the point, in the base of a point, alongside a point, or below the baseboard underneath the point.

Sectional track This comes ready shaped into straights or curves. It is the track supplied in train sets, but can be added to.

Siding A dead-end section of track that is used to store wagons, carriages or locomotives. A buffer stop is used at its dead end to prevent the rolling stock leaving the track.

Sleepers On the real thing, these will be made of wood, metal or concrete and will be at right angles to the rail, ensuring that the rails are held in place as the train passes. On most track systems, they are moulded from plastic.

- A fibreglass brush for cleaning the rails where the fishplates join and for cleaning the moving and current-conducting parts of the points (especially after weathering).
- Small files for smoothing down the edges of the rails where they have been cut.
- A small pair of pliers for pushing the fishplates on to flexible track and for pushing track pins into the pre-drilled holes in the sleepers.
- A small hammer so as to be able to get between the rails if using track pins to fix the track to the baseboard.
- A track-cleaning block for cleaning the tops of the rails after weathering; can also be used after a period during which the layout has stood idle and maybe gathered dust.
- Track cutters for cutting rails; these can be hand-operated, such as those by Xuron, or a mini-drill with a cutting disc attached.

The above tools are available from Expo, Gaugemaster, Squires, larger model shops and Hobbycraft.

BALLASTING

Few of us are happy to run our models on unballasted track because it looks incomplete and unrealistic. In real life, the majority of railway tracks are ballasted and, as we know, ballast holds the track in place, provides drainage and creates a smooth running surface for the trains. Real ballast is usually gravel or other aggregate. Its colour depends upon the type of stone used and the age of the ballast. Not many of us enjoy the task of ballasting our track, but there are some simple ways to make the job easier and more fun.

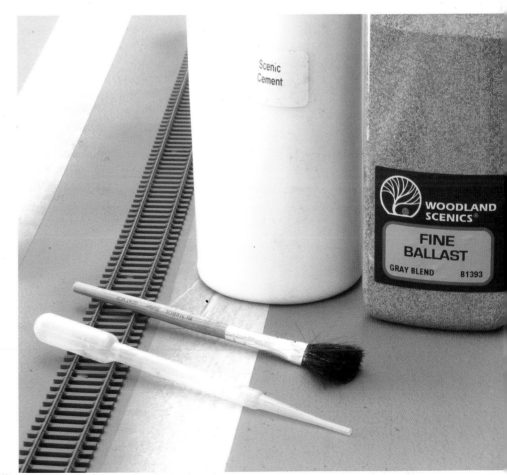

Ballasting with Woodland Scenics Scenic Glue, a brush and a pipette.

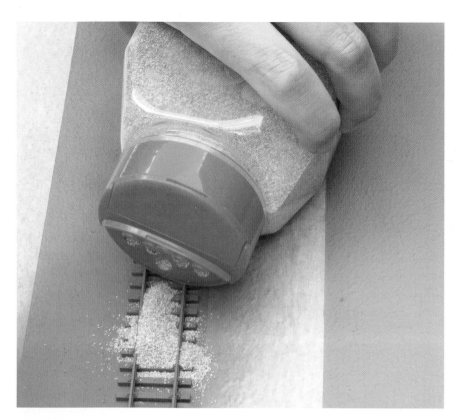

Using a plastic canister to pour the ballast between and outside the rails. It will be necessary to tidy up the ballast with a soft paintbrush after sufficient ballast is tipped on to the track.

Spreading glue on to the spread ballast using a pipette. Do this carefully so as not to disturb the ballast. Experiment with getting the right consistency of the adhesive before starting work on your layout. Diluted PVA works well if it has a few drops of washing-up liquid added to ensure that the adhesive flows easily through the ballast.

CLOCKWISE FROM TOP LEFT:

Removing the masking tape along the side of the track to give a clean edge to the ballast.

There are now a number of specially formulated ballast glues on the market, such as those by Noch and WW Scenics. These run freely through the ballast, thereby making the job quicker.

Super Wet is a US product, which, when added to PVA adhesive, breaks down any resistance in the ballast and aids the free flow of the adhesive.

WHICH TRACK SYSTEMS ARE SOLD READY BALLASTED?

Some manufacturers retail track that is ready ballasted. Whilst the ready-ballasted systems may not look as good as well-ballasted track, with a little weathering they can look quite acceptable. Ready-ballasted track is usually more expensive than unballasted track, but some customers prefer to pay the additional money rather than tackle ballasting themselves.

The current ranges of ready-ballasted track include US manufacturer Atlas, which has a range of ready-ballasted N-scale track. The light colour of the ballast maybe needs to be toned down for UK layouts (go to www.atlasrr.com). The US arm of Bachmann produces a ready-ballasted EZ track range in OO/HO scale and while it needs a bit of weathering to make it look realistic, it could be useful in storage yards (for more information go to www.bachmanntrains.com or www.bachmann.co.uk).

Fleischmann, a German manufacturer, produces the Profi range of ready-ballasted track in both OO/HO and N scales. The Profi track incorporates wood-coloured sleepers with a plastic ballast surround. The compact point motors can be located along the side of the turnouts, alleviating the need to make holes in the baseboard. The points are sold in 'live' frog mode, but the simple removal of wire clips between the tracks converts them into isolating dead frog mode. For more information, go to www.fleischmann.com.

Kato Unitrack has integral ballast in both OO/HO and N scales. The track allows point motors to be fitted under the points. There are also numerous additional items, such as bridges and incline piers, buildings etc. For more information, go to www.katousa.com, or to the distributor in the UK, www.gaugemaster.com.

The HO range of Märklin track uses a third-rail system. Locomotives pick up the electrical current from small stud contacts located in the centre of the sleepers. Märklin's advertising literature claims that 'this third "rail" eliminates polarity problems in wiring, and ensures reliable electrical pickup from the track to the locomotive'. A two-rail version of

the ready-ballasted track by Trix is also available. For more information, go to www.maerklin.com.

Roco's wide range of ready-ballasted HO GeoLine Code 83 track conceals the point motors in its grey ballast base. Both sectional and flexible track are available with a choice of points and crossings. Roco track is also sold in unballasted form. For more information go to www.roco.cc, or to the UK distributor, Gaugemaster.

A BASE FOR THE TRACK

Some modellers choose not to fix the track directly to the baseboard because it means that the trains run more noisily. There are various methods for ameliorating this, including:

• A layer of cork beneath the track allows prototypical deep ballasting for main-line sections of a layout. Various companies, including Gaugemaster, retail strips of cork sheet with angled edges to reflect the shape of ballast. The cork needs to be fixed to the baseboard, then the track fixed to the cork. The next stage is to use fine granite chippings with woodworking PVA glue to model the ballast.

• Woodland Scenics Track-Bed Rolls can be laid in one continuous section, or cut to fit any area. For tight curves, it is recommended to separate Track-Bed along the centre seam, then butt the two pieces snugly. The company also produces a 'Track-Bed Super Sheet', which is ideal for multi-track yards and in multiple sidings. This black lightweight material absorbs the noise of passing trains.

• Peco and other companies sell foam underlay for a quick and easy way to ballast the track. They retail both rolls of plain track foam and designated pieces for specific point sizes. This method offers quieter running characteristics compared to track pinned directly to a wooden baseboard. The one disadvantage of foam underlay is that it has a limited life of about ten years.

• Gaugemaster and Noch produce ballast underlays for both OO and N scales. These are different from normal foam underlays because they have real

Proses' cork underlay is sold in pre-cut pieces, which is a good way to add a layer of cork beneath the track.

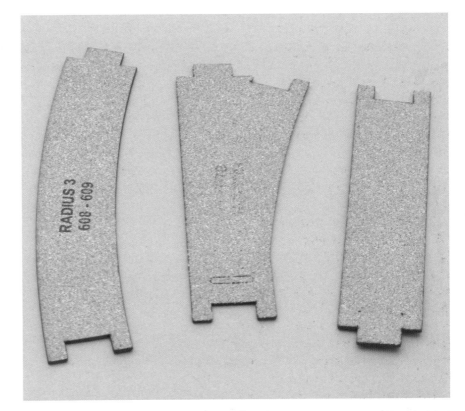

Peco foam underlay provides a neat edge to the foam ballast and trains run quietly on it. For some people, however, it does not look realistic enough and it does have a limited life.

Gaugemaster foam underlay is sold for N and OO track. It has tiny ballast particles embedded in the foam. The underlay is sold in rolls for plain track. For points a kit is available, though another method is to shape pieces of cut underlay for beneath the points.

granite stone bonded to the shoulders and top of the foam. The track slots into the pre-moulded recess, which is simple to do. The OO-scale range features special packs for the points.

• Tillig produces Stryostone trackbedding in brown and light grey colours. It is fitted to the track with the aid of a hair dryer. It is retailed in both rolls and specific sections for points.

BALLASTING, THE COMMON METHOD

Poor ballasting of plain track and the points will not look realistic and may cause running problems. It is important that ballasting is carried out tidily and with care. As noted above, if you are not happy to ballast your track, consider using one of the ready-ballasted track ranges or the foam-strip ballast system.

The most common method of ballasting model track is to use fine stone chippings fixed with slightly diluted PVA adhesive. The disadvantage of this method is that it can make the passing of trains quite noisy and the mixture of fine chippings and PVA around points can create operational trouble unless the ballasting is done very carefully. That said, the results using this method can be visually superb. Ballast is available from a number of companies, including: Busch; C&L; Geoscenics; Noch; Treemendus; Woodland Scenics and WW Scenics. It is sold in a number of colours and sizes suitable for both smaller and larger scales.

One method of keeping the ballasting tidy is to run a length of masking tape on both sides of the track before you start work. Upon completion of the ballasting, removal of the tape should reveal a tidy line along the side of the track. Gently pour ballast on to the centre and sides of the track with an old spoon. Next, use a soft, wide paintbrush to sweep the ballast evenly in-between the sleepers. Clean up any odd granules of ballast left on the sleepers by tapping the rails gently with a screwdriver or craft knife handle. This will settle the ballast between the sleepers.

Use slightly diluted woodworking PVA glue with a wetting agent such as a spray of water mixed with a few drops of washing-up liquid to allow a free flow of the adhesive through the ballast.

Alternatively, there are now dedicated ballast glues on the market that have been prepared to flow quickly and easily through the ballast. Two dedicated ballast glues, one from Noch and the other from WW Scenics, work superbly. They filter through ballast quickly and leave it undisturbed.

BALLASTING WITH A SPREADING TOOL

There are a number of companies that now make ballast-spreading devices. A plastic hopper with a slot dispenses a steady flow of ballast as the tool is dragged along the track. It will work on both straight and curved track, but cannot be used on points or crossings, so the more usual 'by hand' method then needs to be undertaken. If you have lots of plain track to be ballasted, these are useful tools in cutting down the time needed to be spent on ballasting. All of the devices work in roughly the same way:

- Place the ballast spreader over the rails of the track so that it can slide easily, then fill the hopper about two-thirds with ballast.
- Pull the device smoothly along the track in a steady motion. The ballast will fall between the sleepers and along the side of the track; refill the ballast spreader as necessary.
- Once you have finished the section to be ballasted, carefully remove the device from the track so as to spill as little surplus ballast as possible.
- Clean up any odd granules of ballast left on the sleepers by initially tapping the rails gently with a screwdriver or craft knife handle. This will settle the ballast. Use a soft, wide paintbrush to sweep off any leftover pieces of ballast.
- Either lightly spray the ballast with some water containing a couple of drops of washing-up liquid

and then apply a 50/50 PVA glue/water mix through a pipette, or use a dedicated ballast glue such as those by Noch or WW Scenics.

Each manufacturer's ballasting tool is slightly different, so I suggest practising on a plain piece of track before using it to lay ballast on your layout. It takes a little practice to move the spreader at the correct speed to deliver the right amount of ballast in a steady movement. If your hand movement is not steady, the resultant ballast will not be even.

There are YouTube videos demonstrating the best techniques for using these devices, which can be accessed by typing Ballast Spreader into the YouTube search. Gravelboy ballast spreaders from DCC Train Automation come in a number of gauges from Z to O. Ballast Mate by Green Scene is available in N, TT, HOm, EM, P4, OO, O and S scales. Proses' ballast spreader is available from Ontracks and is for N, OO and O scales. Light Work produces spreaders that usefully hold the most ballast. They range in price from around £13 to £20.

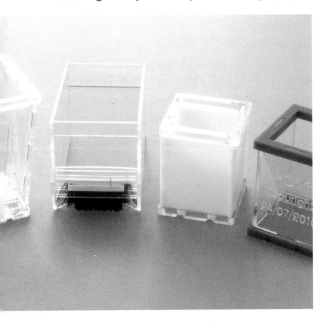

The number of available ballast spreaders is growing. There are at least four for OO-scale track. Some can control the amount of ballast that falls on to the track as it is moved along.

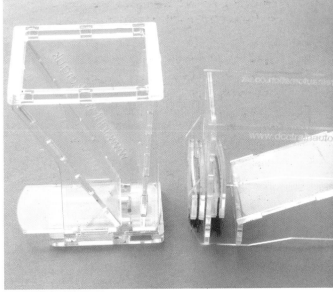

These two ballast spreaders are by Light Work and DCC Automation. Ballast spreaders are available for a large number of track gauges.

Drag the ballast spreader steadily along the track. Do a dry run without ballast first to see how much pressure you need to use to move the spreader. Too much pressure and it will move too quickly; too little and it will not drop enough ballast. Moving the spreader jerkily will not give an even flow of ballast.

Load the spreader carefully so as not to spill any excess on to the layout.

The spreader will drop ballast on to the track both centrally and along the sides of the track.

The points need ballast to be carefully added using an old teaspoon.

After there is sufficient ballast between and outside the rails, sweep out the parts of the points that do not need to be ballasted with a soft paintbrush.

Use the handle of a screwdriver or a craft knife to tap the rails; this will settle the ballast between the sleepers.

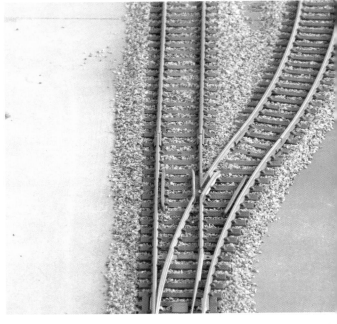

Before fixing down the ballast with adhesive, test the points to ensure that they will move freely.

The finished result – ballasting this section of track took around ten minutes.

TOOLS AND MATERIALS

Tools and materials needed for ballasting consist of:

- Diluted PVA adhesive for fixing down ballast; alternatively, Woodland Scenics Scenic Cement is one of the many products that can be used for this purpose.
- Masking tape for shielding the moving and current-carrying parts of the points when spray-weathering the points.
- Plastic pipette or syringe for dribbling diluted adhesive through the ballast.
- Tacky Glue, which can be rubbed on to the working parts of the point before beginning the ballasting process. This will stop any PVA adhesive sticking the parts of the point that need to be free to move. Alternatively, grease can be used and then removed after the adhesive has fully dried.

- Washing-up liquid – adding a few drops to the PVA will ensure that the diluted PVA flows readily throughout the ballast.
- A wide, soft paintbrush for spreading the ballast evenly along the track and points.

WEATHERING THE TRACK

The rails of new track are far too shiny and for realism it is best to weather the rails once the track has been laid. Arguably, this is better done after ballasting so that both the ballast and rails can be weathered at the same time. Weathering the track can be one of the last jobs to do when building a model railway, but it may be necessary to bring it forward in the order of building if accessibility to the track will be hampered by buildings, trees, fences, signals, catenary masts, bridges and so on.

David Brown's N scale layout features weathered ready ballasted track by Atlas. It is intended to represent the Cornish location at Golant. CHRIS NEVARD/MODEL RAIL

There are several common methods of track weathering, including brush-painting the rails, using an airbrush or aerosol, or using the Rusty Rails Painter tool.

Brush painting the rails This requires three materials: a paintbrush of no greater width than 3mm; a track- cleaning block; and acrylic paints in various colours. Use the brush to apply a dark-brown rusty coloured paint along the rail sides. Because the rail is metal, it may be necessary to apply a second coat where the first coat may not have fully adhered. Paint the rails in sections, trying not to get too much paint on the ballast and sleepers. A thin wash of light-brown plus grey acrylic paint can be brushed along the sleepers and ballast edges after the rails have been painted, if desired.

Remember to try not to paint the contact areas of the rails on the points. If any paint gets into these areas, use a damp cloth to remove it as soon as possible. As the paint is drying, use a track-cleaning block to clean the top and inner edge of the rails. This brush-on method requires a little patience, but by working at it systematically quite a lot can be accomplished in a short time. Suitable acrylic paints are available from Humbrol, Tamiya or any art shop.

Aerosol/airbrush spray method This gives perhaps a slightly better result, but masking out the contact sections on the points and the surrounding land is required in order to limit the weathering to the track. I have found that using an aerosol can be a quicker method to weather long lengths of track, but where there are points it is best to use a paintbrush to weather the track. Various companies retail suitable aerosols, including Humbrol and Phoenix Precision.

The quickest method to weather track is to use an airbrush or an aerosol of matt acrylic paint such as by Humbrol or Phoenix Precision. Use light passes along the track from both sides. Mask off the parts of the points that need to be kept clean to allow the flow of electrical current.

To weather the sides of the rails use a small paintbrush and acrylic paint. This does take quite a bit of time and patience.

The Rusty Rails Painter tool This is an American device consisting of a bottle with a small paint roller at the end of a metal 'arm' for painting matt acrylic paints directly on to the side of the rails. It comes with various discs so that it is suitable to be used for N- and OO/HO-scale track. The top of the bottle is unscrewed and paint is poured into the glass jar.

After the top is screwed back on, the bottle can be tipped on to its side so that the roller can be run along the side of the track. Paint is then drawn through the tube and on to the tiny foam roller. The company has formulated matt acrylic paint in various colours, including weather black, shale, dark brown and brown rust.

Rusty Rails Painter is a tool from the USA that allows a steady flow of paint via a roller wheel on to the side of the rails.

When weathering track, be careful to keep the contact points on the turnouts free of paint. Ensure that the rail surface is thoroughly cleaned after weathering.

Once the points have been laid and ballasted, clean the top of the rails thoroughly using one of the track-cleaning blocks or a fibreglass brush. Both the top surface and the inside top edge of all the running rails must be shiny clean.

Masking the parts of the points that carry the current is essential when weathering the track with an airbrush or aerosol. Here, lengths of Tamiya masking tape have been positioned where it is essential that the rails remain clear of paint.

Just two of various suitable aerosols for track weathering are by Humbrol and Phoenix Precision.

CHAPTER EIGHT

TRAIN CONTROL

Controlling trains has never been so much fun in the history of the hobby.

DCC VERSUS DC TRAIN CONTROL

Whilst many railway modellers use DCC (Digital Command Control) to control their trains, there are still many modellers happily operating their trains using the 'traditional' DC (Direct Current) system. DC is still very popular with beginners and model railway stalwarts alike.

DC control is commonly known as analogue control to differentiate it from DCC. DC is the conventional track-voltage control system that typically provides between 0V and 12V DC for train speed control and polarity reversal for direction control. There are two components to train control using DC – a transformer and the speed-control equipment. Transformers change the voltage of an AC (alternating current) supply to DC. A transformer is either part of the control unit (an integrated unit), or a separate item either for track and accessory power (for example, point motors). A 'cut-out' protective overload device is usually built into the controller.

These reset automatically when the cause of the overload is removed.

Some controllers feature 'inertia' or 'momentum' control. This allows the operator to accelerate a train automatically, as well as allowing it to coast or be braked to a standstill, giving more realistic acceleration and braking. Feedback controllers create a closed loop between the controller and the locomotive that senses the load in the circuit and constantly adjusts the output. This helps to maintain the locomotive at an even speed up and down gradients. Feedback controllers are not suitable for all types of locomotive, so you need to study the locomotive instructions accordingly.

Basic train-set controllers are fine for small layouts, but when you choose to expand a layout it may be best to look towards the specialist manufacturers such as Gaugemaster and All Components (www.allcomponents.co.uk) for your equipment. A quick glance at their websites will reveal that they produce a large number of products that are targeted at specific layouts and scales – for example, they will recom-

DCC is one of the hobby's recent developments that can add such a lot to the enjoyment of the running of the trains. Here a Gaugemaster Prodigy system is being used.

mend different controllers depending upon whether the layout is N, OO or O scale. These companies also produce transformers just for accessories, as well as a whole range of other electrical equipment. The Gaugemaster website has a lot of useful general information about both DC controllers and DCC. Go to the left-hand bar on www.gaugemaster.com.

Train control is a lot more fun than ever using DCC. DCC systems range from the simple to use to as challenging as you would like. There are starter DCC systems for small layouts that do not cost the earth. DCC control is also available in wireless mode. Some who were reluctant for years to begin using DCC have now tried it and say they would find it difficult to go back to DC operation. Constant bright lighting on the locomotives is just one of the advantages of DCC operation.

Many ready-to-run locomotives are now available as: DCC-ready (these need a decoder to be fitted, but already have a pin connection to take the decoder); DCC-fitted (already fitted with a decoder); or DCC-sound (fitted with decoder, a sound chip and a loudspeaker).

THE PROS AND CONS OF USING DCC

DCC arrived in the model railway hobby back in the 1980s and now most of the mainstream manufacturers produce DCC systems together with locomotives and multiple units being sold already fitted with a decoder and maybe a loudspeaker.

Many modellers have already gone down the DCC route, but some are still sitting on the fence wondering if they should go DCC, while a small number are determined not to change from DC. At model railway shows, visitors watch DCC-fitted locos working on a layout. They hear the apparent opening and closing of the cab doors, the lights go on and off, the sound of the squealing brakes and the build-up of the power. Some think these benefits of DCC are worth the additional cost. Other modellers are happy to carry on as they are with analogue train operation.

The cons The cost element comes to mind initially. How much would it cost to fit a decoder to all the

locomotives on a layout? But is that really necessary? DCC sound-fitted locomotives cost nearly twice as much as non-DCC sound-fitted locomotives. Some modellers would prefer to have fewer locomotives in order to have them all sound-fitted, while others would prefer to have more locomotives and not have them all sound-fitted.

Some modellers may feel that they lack confidence about electrical matters, so think that DCC is an unnecessary complication for their layout and they may not have the enthusiasm to spend the time researching DCC and its possibilities. Modellers sometimes look at DCC controllers that have rows of buttons and are put off because it all looks too daunting to learn. DCC instruction manuals look inaccessible to many casual readers and those of us who do like the look of technical handbooks could be put off by the apparent complexity of it all. When potential customers hear about 6-pin, 8-pin and 21-pin plugs they just do not know which is best for their locomotives and fear they never will.

Bachmann DCC-fitted Class 25 locomotive with the headcode lights illuminated.

Bachmann DCC-fitted Class 25 locomotive with the tail lights illuminated.

The pros The benefits of DCC are available to all. It really is not that complicated, can be learnt quite quickly and is certainly fun to use. DCC starter train sets including the DCC system are remarkable value for money and contain everything that you need to get started. Wiring a layout can potentially be easier with DCC. To maintain enthusiasm for the hobby, it is often good to have a new challenge. Why not let DCC be your next challenge?

To run trains with sound, including locomotive sounds, platform announcements, squealing brakes, horns and much more can be a lot of fun. Locomotive lights stay brightly lit rather than fading as a locomotive stops. DCC is definitely one of the most exciting things to happen in model railways for a long time. It has many advantages over traditional DC control and whilst there is an additional cost for each locomotive, many modellers think that the cost is worth it because of the better loco control and additional features.

The future looks bright for DCC developments. Each year new products and innovations arrive on the market and there are an increasing number of sound-fitted locomotives being offered by UK manufacturers. Hornby has introduced its RailMaster system using the Elite DCC system and a PC or laptop. The program provides for any number of locomotives to be given tailored default settings to suit individual models, including slow speed running, cruising speed, direction lights and so on. RailMaster also supports DCC sound locomotives, plus it is simple to program locomotives so that they will follow a series of commands automatically.

Decoders can be programmed to adjust the rates of acceleration and deceleration, the volume of the speakers and much more. None of this is usually necessary, however, because the factory-fitted settings usually work just fine. Whilst a DCC system allows us to operate locomotives and their functions, it also enables us to control other devices on the layout such as points. But you can choose to leave these operated by DC if you prefer.

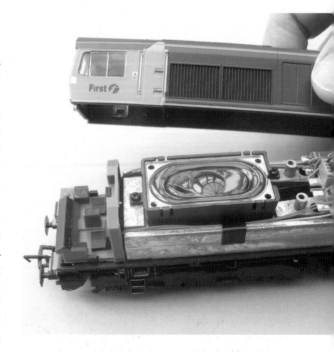

Lifting the lid on a Bachmann Class 66 DCC Sound loco. The large loudspeaker is seen to the left on the top of the chassis.

DCC sound systems can be purchased separately from a number of companies. They retail at around £100 to include the DCC decoder, the wiring and the loudspeaker.

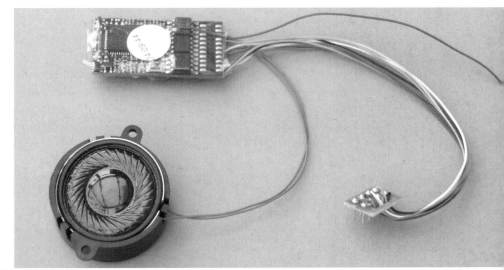

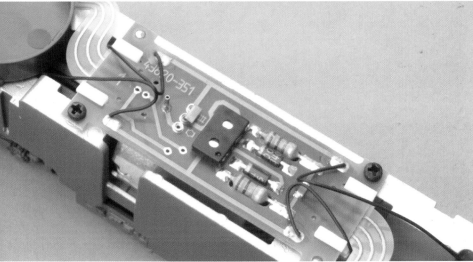

When a DC locomotive is taken out of the box it usually has a DCC blanking-off plate installed, as can be seen here as the black plastic rectangular piece on top of the chassis.

To install a decoder into the locomotive, remove the blanking plate. On this locomotive there are eight pins to hold the decoder. Increasingly, on OO locomotives there are 21-pin decoders.

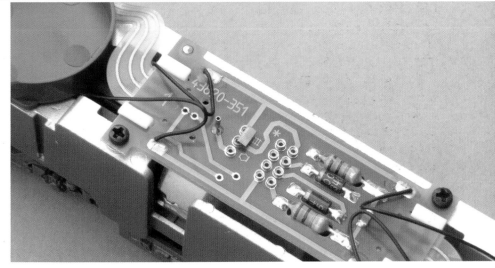

If you intend to run a layout frequently, the DCC learning curve will be steep, but it will soon reach a plateau that will make operation quick and easy. DCC is definitely fun to use and adds lots of additional operating features to the hobby. Those who 'go DCC' rarely regret it.

SETTING A LIMIT ON THE COST

If you are concerned that the costs of DCC might spiral, set yourself a limit on the number of locomotives you will equip with DCC so as to limit the outlay. Just fit sound into your favourite locomotives. Maybe limit to how much you want to spend on DCC equipment, including decoders. If you have a small layout, one of the basic DCC systems in the starter sets by Bachmann or Hornby might be adequate to get the benefits of DCC. Or if you are about to take the first step of DCC, why not just use it in a goods yard with a few decoder-installed locomotives to keep the initial cost down as you learn how to get the most out of it?

WHAT SYSTEM SHOULD I BUY?

If you are wondering whether to buy a complex or basic DCC system, you may want to ask yourself the following questions:

• How often do I usually operate my layout and is operation my main interest in the hobby?
• How many DCC locomotives do I intend to use?
• Is the layout large or compact and do I intend to control accessories such as point motors by DCC?

The more often that you operate your layout and the larger the layout is, the more you should lean towards buying one of the more powerful DCC systems. If the layout is large, you may need a lot of current to the track, so choose a system that has a high number of amps and booster equipment from its power source. The same applies if you want to use DCC to operate point motors and so on.

If you only run your layout occasionally, you might find that you have to get the manual out every time you do use it in order to familiarize yourself once more with how to do it. In that

Tips for DCC Control

• Do not be tempted to buy the first system you see. Do your research and think carefully about your requirements – are you going to run lots of DCC-equipped locomotives and/or accessories, or just a few? DCC systems vary in price and specification and it is best to get the choice of system right first time.

• Talk to manufacturers, retailers and other DCC users at model railway shows to see which is the best system for you and your layout. Ask layout operators at shows what they like about DCC. And what they do not like!

• Read the instruction manual of the system that you buy. Do not expect to understand and remember it all at first reading. It takes time to become familiar with a DCC system. But stick at it and you will be surprised at how much DCC can do for your layout.

• Start simply by exploring DCC thoroughly with just one locomotive so as to give yourself a full grounding of its potential. Standardize your equipment where possible. For example, use all the same control equipment so that it will be compatible. Use decoders that you are happy with and have learnt to work with.

• Ideally, all the wiring connections and the rail joints of a layout should be soldered. Keep the locomotive wheels and the track as clean as possible.

• Do not be tempted to 'play around' with modifying decoder settings to begin with. If you choose to modify them later on, it is best to work methodically, recording the changes and observing the effects of each change that you make.

• Take your time! Enjoy DCC. Just remember it's fun.

A Dapol Class 22 locomotive reaches the top of the climb on the author's Holcombe branch line. CHRIS NEVARD/ MODEL RAIL

The Bachmann DCC EZ controller is a good starter system. The wiring demonstrated in the picture is basic DCC wiring, which is certainly not complex for a small layout. Larger layouts may require additional power-bus wiring around the layout.

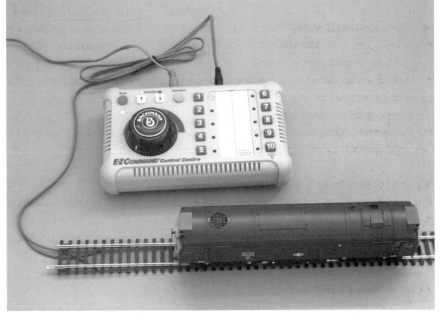

case, it may be best to buy a basic system. Some DCC controllers/throttles/cabs are hand-held, while some are designed for panel mounting. Others provide wireless hand-held controllers. The choice is usually down to what controller you most prefer to use.

CHAPTER NINE

IMPROVING ROLLING STOCK

One hour spent detailing a locomotive makes a big difference to the look of the model.

Locomotive models in all scales run better now than at any time in the history of the hobby. This applies to steam, electric and diesel locomotives. All-wheel electrical pick-up is now increasingly common on locomotives. Models run much more quietly and smoothly than they did some years ago. The days of stalling over the points are fading fast if the track is kept clean.

Rolling stock and locomotives are now very well detailed in all scales. Paint finish, lining, numbering and the application of liveries is generally very good indeed. Flush glazing is now common and rolling stock is available in weathered or unweathered finishes.

ADDING THE DETAILS

Many of today's diesel, electric and steam locomotives arrive with a small plastic bag containing detailing parts to be fitted by the purchaser. Some purchasers choose to fit the detailing parts to their locomotives, while others do not. In this section, we show that it is fun to fit the parts and the models look so much better as a result of an hour or so of work. The more nimble one's fingers, the better for this task.

Whilst most collectors and modellers agree that the locomotives do look better with the parts attached, there are various reasons why purchasers

A locomotive that has been improved by a light pass of acrylic paint from a Humbrol aerosol.

The level of minute details on today's models is superb. This is the destination board on a Rivarrossi HO-scale model of a TEE Gotthardo electric multiple unit.

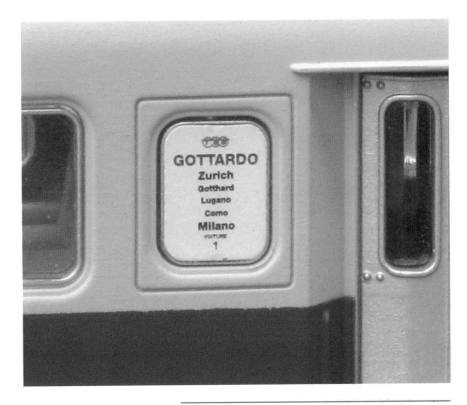

decide not to fit them. Collectors of locomotives prefer to keep their models in 'mint and boxed' condition. Some modellers choose to operate their locomotives with tension-lock couplings on both ends of a model for easy shunting. If the tension-lock couplings are left on the locomotives, it is generally not possible to add all the detailing parts. Some of the parts are rather fiddly to fit and thus some modellers consider that the effort of adding them is not worth the trouble.

Locomotives come with a different array of add-on parts. For example, a Bachmann 'Thunderbirds' Class 57 locomotive comes with the following additional parts to be fitted: two nameplates; two roof aerials; and six pipes for each cab end. A Bachmann Collectors Club Class 85 locomotive comes with five detailing pieces to be added on each end, plus nameplates and depot plaques.

For the purpose of this chapter, a Hornby Colas Class 66 locomotive and a Bachmann Class 85 locomotive are used to illustrate the techniques. Similar methods can be used for diesel, electric and steam locomotives.

DETAILING THE LOCOMOTIVE

The first task is to look carefully at the leaflet showing the assembly details of the particular locomotive. Get familiar with the instructions before you start work on the detailing process. Locomotive models have various small holes in the buffer beam, cab front, cab roof and bogie to push the parts into. Not all locomotives have the same number of holes or bits and pieces to add. At its simplest, it is just a matter of pushing the right detailing part into the right hole.

Work out the order in which you will add the parts to the locomotive, so that the parts you fit first will not obscure your view when working with the other parts. Work on one end of a locomotive at a time. If the detailing parts come on a plastic sprue, cut the appropriate number of parts from the sprue using a sharp craft knife over a self-sealing cutting board. Put the tiny pieces aside in the order that you will fix them to the locomotive.

Use a pair of fine-nosed tweezers to hold the piece and push the 'plug' on each part into the correct hole. Sometimes it is possible to use your fingers to do this instead of the tweezers. Occasionally, I find that some of the holes on the locomotive are a little on the tight side and need to be expanded with a very small diameter file. Another way of doing this is to remove carefully a little plastic from the 'plug' on the part with a sharp craft knife or a small file. Ensure that the 'plug' is pushed well into its hole, then dab a little plastic cement on to the join with a small, fine paintbrush to make it secure.

When the pipes are fixed firmly to the locomotive – the adhesive usually dries in well under an hour – the connections on the pipes can be highlighted using yellow or orange acrylic paint as appropriate. Look at photos of the real thing to see which pipes are painted which colour. Some of the more recent locomotives come with ready-painted pipe connections, which saves time. Adding the roof-mounted air horns and hood-mounted aerials (if supplied) is simply done by putting a little plastic cement into the hole with a very fine paintbrush, then pushing home the aerials (be careful that they are vertical) and horns.

The purchaser can choose whether he wants to fit the parts on both ends, or just one. Many modellers choose to detail just one end of the locomotive and leave the tension-lock coupling on the other end. Sometimes the add-on plastic parts are made from shiny plastic that might benefit from a little repainting with matt acrylic paint, or weathering with chalks or aerosols or airbrushing.

Where manufacturers supply nameplates, they sometimes usefully print a location guide on the side of the locomotive. These guides make the fitting of nameplates a lot easier. It is necessary carefully to cut the nameplates from the metal strip, then fix the plate to the locomotive side with a small amount of superglue.

This detailing work on one end of a locomotive usually takes about one hour. I have found that locomotives with the detailing parts added give a lot of satisfaction to the person who has done the work. Go on, give it a go!

WHAT SKILLS ARE NEEDED?

A little bit of patience is needed to read the instructions thoroughly rather than rushing ahead and fitting a part in the wrong position on the locomotive, then having to remove it after the glue has dried. Learning which pipes go where is best done by looking at photos of the real thing.

A steady hand is required to position the add-on parts. You may find that one of those fixed magnifying glasses works well when doing this. You must be able to work with small drops of adhesive to ensure that it does not get on to other parts of the model and also be able to paint carefully with micro-paintbrushes, masking other parts of the model where corrective painting or varnishing is necessary. Small drills are required for drilling out holes in the buffer beam that need to be opened up a little to take the add-on parts. Working with very small parts can be learnt and tweezers are useful for doing this.

TOOLS AND MATERIALS

Tools and materials needed for adding loco details consist of:

• Acrylic paint (black, yellow, orange, red) where the details come unpainted.
• A magnifying glass.

A selection of four pairs of tweezers and a craft knife for work with locomotive add-on parts.

- Matt varnish.
- Plastic cement.
- A self-sealing cutting board.
- Set of various pairs of small tweezers.
- A sharp craft knife.
- A small file.
- Small paintbrushes for painting and for use with plastic cement.
- Weathering chalks for toning down any shiny parts.

WHERE TO GET MORE INFORMATION

Most manufacturers supply a pictorial guide with each locomotive, showing where the parts are to be inserted on each of their models. The Bachmann website, for example, features its instruction leaflets at: http://bachmann.co.uk/service/assmbly.php.

Before starting work on detailing any locomotive, it is worth referring to the various prototype motive-power books and magazines that are available. These books contain illustrations showing where to fix the various pipes, nameplates, air horns, buffer-bar details and so on. These include Cades Locomotive Guide, which provides information about all British outline models (for more information, see www.cadeslocomotiveguide.co.uk) and the Modern Locomotive Illustrated series (www.mli-magazine.com), which contains good pictures of buffer-beam details.

A Heljan OO-scale Class 26 locomotive with all the buffer-beam details fitted.

The front end of a Hornby OO-scale Colas Class 66 locomotive straight out of the box. Note the tension-lock coupling, holes in the buffer beam and cutaway snowplough/ obstacle deflector.

The first step is to remove the cutaway lower front plate, which is a 'push-on' feature. The lower front end plates that are fitted to the locomotive enable a tension-lock coupling to be used on both ends of the locomotive. By removing this and fitting the full one, you will no longer be able to use tension-lock couplings.

There are the four add-on parts – three pipes and one full-front lower plate that are all moulded in black plastic.

Next, slide the coupling upwards out of its 'box'. The coupling is not glued in, so it is quite easy to remove.

Here is the front of the locomotive after fitment of the detailing parts.

IMPROVING THE LOOK OF A DMU

This project required very little time, money and expertise, but really improved the look of a ready-to-run diesel multiple unit (DMU). Similar techniques can be applied to other items of rolling stock. I used a Hornby OO-scale London Midland refurbished Class 153 single-car DMU model as the basis for this project. This model is available in a number of liveries in OO scale

and a model of the Class 153 unit is available in N scale by Dapol.

London Midland's fleet of single-car DMU Class 153s has been used extensively on the Coventry to Nuneaton line and between Bedford and Bletchley. Some of these units were cascaded to Devon and Cornwall, so LM-liveried units have been seen running in the West Country too. The units were upgraded by Wabtec Ltd at Eastleigh to include better cycle storage, information screens and CCTV, in addition to interior and exterior refurbishment.

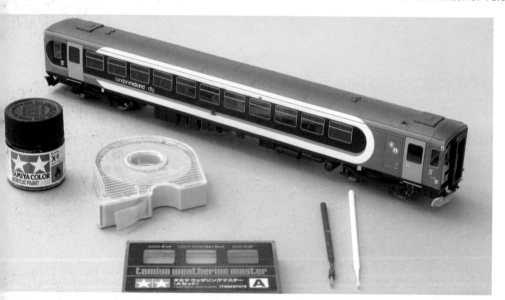

A Hornby London Midland Class 153 unit before work on it commences. The black Tamiya paint will be used to paint the edges of the snowploughs and the masking tape used lightly to protect other parts of the model when painting is under way. There are weathering chalks and applicator by Tamiya, as well as micro-brushes to be used for the fine painting.

London Midland Class 153 354 at Woburn Sands station on its journey from Bedford to Bletchley on 22 September 2010.

For this quick project, these materials were used: matt black Tamiya paint to paint the edges of the snowploughs/obstacle deflectors; masking tape to protect lightly other parts of the model when painting and weathering; weathering chalks and the supplied applicator by Tamiya for the dusty effects; and micro-brushes for fine painting.

The first time I saw the Hornby Class 153 model I thought that the thickness of the plastic snowplough (or obstacle deflector) marred the look of the model,

so I set about thinking how to remedy this. I used a micro-paintbrush to paint the flat edges of the snowplough black, which certainly went some way to disguise the thickness of the plastic moulding. I also weathered and added dust to the snowplough and grilles and details on the lower bodywork using a Tamiya foam applicator to rub on the chalk. I used the other end of the Tamiya applicator to brush off any excess chalk. The result is so much more realistic than shiny plastic.

CLOCKWISE FROM TOP LEFT:

A view of a pristine Hornby Class 153 London Midland single-car DMU. In my view, the thickness of the snowplough mars the look of the model, but it is quite easy to remedy this.

Using a micro-paintbrush to paint the edge of the snowplough. This is arguably the trickiest part of the process, but with a steady hand each end is only a five-minute job.

Here is the snowplough after painting and weathering. The thickness of the plastic is definitely not so obvious now and the weathering makes the front end of the DMU look better.

To weather and add dust to the grilles and details on the lower bodywork, I used a Tamiya foam applicator to rub on the chalk.

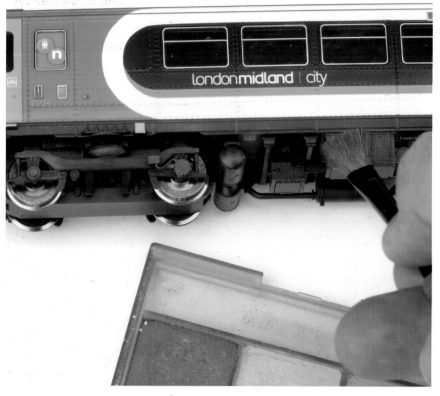

I used the other end of the Tamiya applicator to brush off any excess chalk. If you are not using Tamiya weathering chalks, alternatives to their supplied tool are make-up removal 'tools', which are basically a little foam cap on the end of a piece of short plastic and a soft paintbrush.

Here is the effect after the chalk has been applied. It looks much more realistic than shiny black plastic.

The front of the unit shows the more discreet snowplough, some weathering around the corridor connection and the general light weathering.

An overall view of the Hornby Class 153 unit after it has been 'toned down' by light weathering on the lower body side.

On the ends of the unit I also weathered the door frames with weathering chalk to give the illusion of gathering dirt from the air as the unit travelled along. Finally, weathering chalk was lightly rubbed along the roof too, so that any shine on the model was removed.

The work on the unit took around an hour and cost less than £1 and I am now so much more pleased with the model. I could have gone on to make other adjustments, like fitting a finer-scale replacement snowplough and using matt or satin acrylic varnish aerosol to finish off the model, but I was content with the model after the changes I had made. I thoroughly recommend George Dent's excellent *Detailing and Modifying Ready-to-Run Locomotives in OO Gauge* books published by Crowood for more information on improving locomotives.

THE SKILLS REQUIRED

This really is a beginner's project and requires just looking at the real thing to see what improvements are possible, then painting with a fine brush and weathering with chalks.

TOOLS AND MATERIALS

Tools required for improving the look of a DMU consist of:

- Black acrylic or enamel paint.
- Low-tack masking tape to protect the model during painting.
- Micro-paintbrushes.
- Weathering chalks with applicator or a cotton bud and soft paintbrush.

Handling the small add-on parts becomes easier after you have decided which pair of tweezers suits you best.

Micro-paintbrushes are really useful for this type of work because they can supply small amounts of paint in a precise way.

A SIMPLE LOCOMOTIVE MAKEOVER

The Bachmann USA OO-scale model of Toby looks rather toy-like, but it can be worked on to improve its realism.

Toby, as seen in the previous picture, after some detailing, repainting and weathering. Though its toy origin is still evident, it does give a fairly decent representation of an LNER Tram locomotive.

DETAILING A BACHMANN CLASS 85 LOCOMOTIVE

A Bachmann Class 85 Collectors' Club locomotive straight out of the box with the small packet of detailing parts to the left and the instruction leaflet.

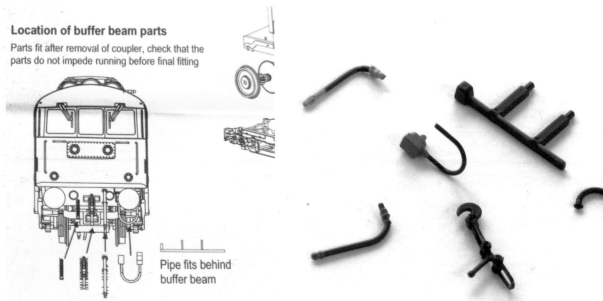

Close-up of the instruction leaflet showing the diagram relating to the fitment of the detailing parts.

These are the six parts to be fitted to each end of the Class 85 locomotive.

The Class 85 as it comes straight out of the box. Note the ready-drilled holes in the buffer beam. If the tension-lock coupling is to be retained, not all of the detailing parts may be added.

Once the parts is added to the buffer beam, drop a small drop of plastic cement on to the join to fix the part firmly to the locomotive.

The Class 85 locomotive with the details added. I used just a couple of drops of Woodland Scenics black colour pigments on the tip of a small paintbrush to hide the excess adhesive on the buffer beam.

CHAPTER TEN

WEATHERING

*Weathering is the process of making models look more realistic by simulating
the effects of rain, sun, dust, snow, grime and ageing.*

Weathering is very much a personal matter. Some of us will understandably choose not to weather our rolling stock because of the possible resale implications. We can choose how far we want to weather our rolling stock – will it be lightly weathered, or very dirty? We can also be selective with our weathering – so, for example, a wagon can be detailed and painted to represent replacement timbers and panels.

Buildings and landscape features can also be weathered in the pursuit of realism. Most of the methods for weathering rolling stock can be used on buildings too. And of course weathered track looks so much better than shiny new rails.

I find it satisfying to see a train working its way around a layout that I have weathered myself. To me, the weathering process is fun, although initially I found the whole process rather worrying. And even now, after weathering numerous things, each time I begin on a new item of rolling stock I still hope that I will make this wagon look better, not worse. But with a little practice almost fail-safe methods can be used, as we will go on to discuss.

WEATHERING TECHNIQUES

The good thing about weathering is that one or more techniques can be used to reach the desired result. Most of the methods are interchangeable and can work well together. For example, a wagon might benefit from just using weathering dyes or

The weathered Bachmann Scenecraft concrete loading works is an ideal corner filler.

Weathering dyes are available from a number of companies. They offer versatile ways of weathering rolling stock and buildings. Being water- or alcohol-soluble, they provide good adhesion even on glossy paint finishes and smooth metals. They can either be sprayed on with an airbrush, or brushed on with a flat paintbrush. They dry with a matt finish.

Enamel light washes are available from AK and Humbrol to be used in the same way as weathering dyes.

chalks. Alternatively, it may also be distressed using a fibreglass brush. To add more variety, it might be distressed with a fibreglass brush, then treated with weathering dyes, then the lower body sprayed with a thin coat of acrylic paint or weathering dyes. The mixture of techniques that can be applied to just one model makes weathering a fun process. It is very much down to the personal preference of the modeller.

TOOLS AND MATERIALS

Tools and materials needed for weathering consist of:

- Aerosols of acrylic paint and matt varnish or an airbrush.
- Fibreglass brushes.
- Matt varnish.
- Old newspaper to put on the table as you work.
- Small paintbrushes for painting on matt varnish, weathering dyes and chalks.
- Weathering chalks and a flat applicator brush.
- Weathering dyes.

It is not necessary to use all of these materials. Weathering is very much a personal matter. It is always best to use what you are most comfortable with and what you are confident at producing good results with.

SPRAYING WITH AIRBRUSH AND AEROSOLS

Airbrushes spray paint in a controlled application. They can be used for spraying large or small areas of paint or varnish and are very good for weathering effects. Spray aerosols are available in matt, satin, gloss, rail, metallic, metalcote, clear and varnish. Some are acrylic and others enamel, but both are good for weathering. Do not hold the spray too close to the model, or the paint will be applied too thickly. Spray the flow of paint slightly down of the model, which will add a fine film of light dust.

DISTRESSING WITH A FIBREGLASS BRUSH

Fibreglass brushes work on the same principle as a propelling pencil, which means that the bristles can be pushed out as demanded. Replacement fibres are available. They are good at 'scratching' the sides of wagons, imitation steel girder bridges and so on to

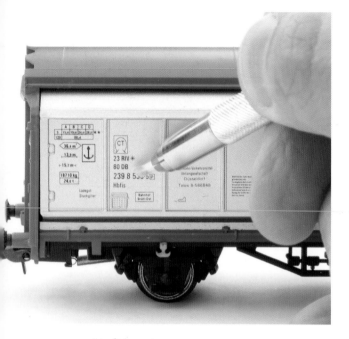

Fibreglass brushes are good for 'scratching' the sides of wagons, imitation steel girder bridges and the like to give a well-worn look. Do not use these tools too aggressively because even one firm stroke can remove the transfer detail from an item of rolling stock. Once the shine of the wagon has gone, weathering chalks can be used.

Before and after... Two identical wagons by Electrotren. The one on the left was weathered initially by distressing with a fibreglass brush, then by adding the rust effects using weathering chalks and dyes.

give a well-worn look. Do not use them too aggressively, because even one firm stroke can remove the transfer detail from an item of rolling stock. Once the shine of the wagon has gone, weathering chalks and other techniques can be used.

Beware – do not to touch the ends of the fibreglass bristles because they can easily get stuck into one's fingers, causing irritation.

USING WEATHERING DYES

Weathering dyes, such as those made by Joe's Model Trains (www.joesmodeltrains.com), are versatile ways of weathering rolling stock and buildings. Weathering dyes are water- or alcohol-soluble and provide good adhesion even on glossy paint finishes and smooth metals. They dry to a matt finish and can be sprayed with an airbrush or brushed on with a flat paintbrush.

Use thin washes of the dyes, starting at the top of the item of rolling stock or building and, as with the other methods, let the diluted dye drip down through the brickwork or motive-power details. If you have used too much, it can be easily washed off the model.

DRY BRUSHING

This method is used to enhance the raised details on a model rather than for applying a solid colour. The technique is as follows: lightly dip a small paintbrush into acrylic or enamel paint, then rub the excess paint off the bristles of the brush on some paper tissue; brush lightly over the details of the wagon so that the paint will stick to the raised details and will highlight them; finally, leave to dry fully before applying other weathering methods.

USING WEATHERING CHALKS

Various companies make weathering chalks in a number of colours. Chalks are available in powder, pan or stick form. It you obtain the stick chalks, grind them to a fine powder over very fine sandpaper.

Humbrol and Tamiya chalks are widely available in model shops in the UK. The Humbrol chalks are sold in small bottles, while the Tamiya chalks are sold in plastic trays of three colours, plus a double-ended

Before... A pristine 'out of the box' PCA wagon from Hornby.

After... The same wagon after weathering, using dyes for the white chemicals and a light brown sweep along the lower half of the body with an aerosol of acrylic paint.

Drybrushing is very useful for accentuating the details on a model. Firstly, a little paint is applied to a paintbrush (by dipping it into the paint), then most of the paint is removed by dragging the brush on a paper tissue. The 'dry' brush can then be moved back and forth across a model with gentle strokes to highlight the raised details.

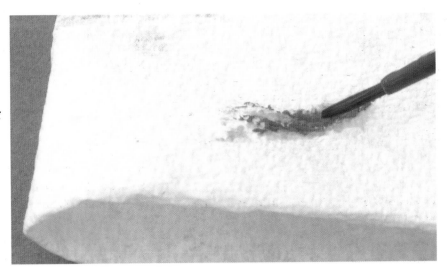

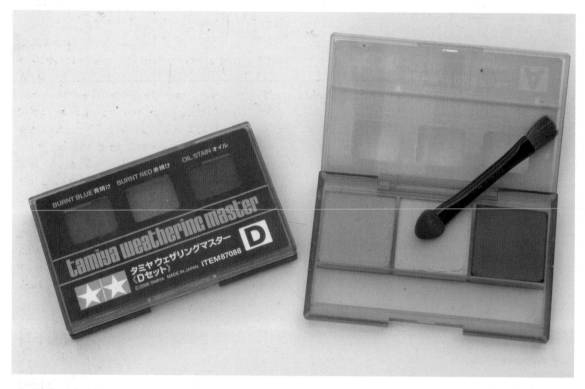

Weathering chalks are available from a number of companies. Here is one of the various plastic trays of three chalks by Tamiya with the supplied applicator.

brush (sponge one end, sponge brush the other) for applying the powdered chalks. Other companies that offer weathering chalks are AK Interactive, Carr's, DCC Concepts, Double O Scenics, Geoscenics, LifeColour, Noch and MIG.

Chalks are finely ground pigments that may be rubbed on to a surface to produce a permanent stain. They can be brushed or rubbed on to the model with a soft paintbrush, a make-up brush, a cotton bud or felt pads. Noch or Tamiya chalks supply a brush with which to collect chalk from the receptacle and then work it into the corners and cracks of a model. Chalks work best when applied to dull or non-glossy models, so you may find that applying a light coating of matt varnish or distressing the model with fibre-glass brushes before weathering will give the chalk more chance to adhere to the model.

The chalks should be rubbed in the direction that the weathering would naturally form. So on a locomotive or a container rain would wash down the sides and hence all of the strokes should be down the sides of the model. The tip of your finger is sometimes a useful tool for spreading chalks and weathering dyes. If you do not like the effect that you have made, the chalk can be wiped away by using a damp cloth.

To create rust spots, mix up a paste consisting of a small amount of chalk and a little matt varnish or PVA glue. Dab the paste on to the sides and under-frame of wagons with a small paintbrush, a wooden stick or a cocktail stick. Drag the paste downwards to create the appearance of streaks of rust washed down the sides of the wagon by rain. Leave to dry before doing any other weathering of the model. Alternatively, paint a few dabs of matt varnish on to the model, then spread the weathering chalk on to the spots of still wet varnish.

When you are happy with the finished result, the weathering can be sealed in and protected by a quick spray of matt varnish from an aerosol. Matt varnish on a weathered model does, however, have the effect of lightening the weathering effect.

WEATHERING RESIN BUILDINGS

Within a few years of a real building being erected, it starts to look a little dirty or tired. A resin building straight out of the box looks good, but can look even better by experimenting with a few simple techniques. Weathering the roof is one of the most important things to do because this will catch the eye first. This can be done using dry brushing.

The walls of a building can be weathered using the same dry brushing technique as described above .Weathering can also be undertaken with an airbrush, charcoal or chalk pastels. Watercolour paints are another cheap and cheerful way to weather these buildings – just running some diluted watercolour paint down through the brick courses is a good way to start.

MAKING AN OTA WAGON LOOK WELL USED

For many years, modellers in OO scale were keen to see OTA wagons being made in ready-to-run form. In 2011–12, two came along from Bachmann and Hornby of different prototypes and both are good representations of the real thing. The Bachmann wagon comes complete with a resin load, but loads have to be bought separately for the Hornby wagon. The wagons require a little assembly to add the side stanchions, but that is a five minute job using a little plastic cement and a micro paintbrush.

In real life, as the accompanying picture shows, OTA wagons were always pretty dirty and 'bashed around' because logs have been loaded on and off them frequently. To make the model wagons look more realistic, some weathering is essential.

Different types of OTA wagons at the timber loading siding at Arrochar and Tarbet on the West Highland Line on 25 September 2006.

The Hornby OTA wagon straight out of the box looks very clean indeed. Nothing like this would be seen on a real railway for more than one day!

I tackled the look of the axle and wheel detail in two stages – first by painting the springs mid-grey with slightly diluted acrylic paint so that it would seep into the detail, then using weathering dyes to add the grubby and tired look to the chassis. The wagon starts to look well used.

After the weathering dyes and chalks had been used, a Bachmann OTA wagon was given a light spray of Humbrol dark brown acrylic. This picture is staged – the aerosol is being held far too close for light weathering of a wagon. It should be held at least twice this distance from the wagon.

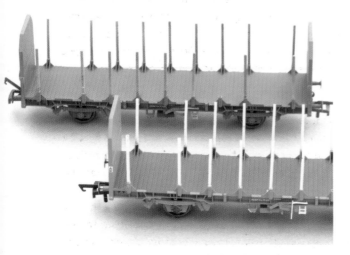

Weathered and unweathered Hornby OTA wagons next to each other for comparison purposes.

The completed Hornby wagon. The strapping in this picture was in hindsight too wide, so it was later replaced with a narrower strap.

This Hornby OTA wagon has intentionally been left without a load. A little Treemendus Forest Floor scatter material was sprinkled on the floor and then diluted PVA adhesive 'flooded' over the floor from a small bottle. When the glue had dried it left white marks, so a quick coat of matt varnish from an aerosol removed all this. The final effect is a wagon waiting to be loaded with lots of tree debris on it.

WEATHERING A CONTAINER

Containers are a very common sight on today's railways. There are approximately seventeen million intermodal containers in the world of varying types to suit different cargoes. Containers are built to standardized dimensions and can be loaded and unloaded, stacked, transported efficiently over long distances and transferred from one mode of transport to another. There are five common standard lengths: 6.1m (20ft); 12.2m (40ft); 13.7m (45ft); 14.6m (48ft); and 16.2m (53ft).

Some containers look new, some are time-weathered, while others look downright rusty. Another visual difference is that some containers carry patches of new paint and data boxes. Look at real containers to see how they age. Take your own photographs of them to refer to as you weather the models.

Weathering a container is a good way to learn the various skills that can then be used on locomotives and items of rolling stock. An airbrush is not required to weather a container. If you want to model a paint-faded container, it can be lightly sprayed using light grey and brown paint from an aerosol. Very light passes from the lower sides of the container are all that is needed. Chalks are very good applied in the direction that the weathering would naturally form. So on a container rain would wash down the sides and hence all the strokes should be down the sides of the container. If you do not like the effect that you have created, the chalk can be wiped away using a damp cloth.

To create spots and areas of concentrated rust, paint on a few dabs of matt varnish and then spread weathering chalk on to the spots. When you are happy with the finished result, the weathering can be sealed in and protected by a quick spray of matt varnish from an aerosol.

These pristine HO-scale Atlas models are standard-height 12.2m (40ft) containers models sold in packs of three. Various company names and liveries are available, including K-Line, Maersk Line, Maersk Sealand and Hanjin. The bodies are well moulded with bevelled corrugated sides. There are separately attached door rods and handles.

Various companies retail weathering chalks. For this project, chalks by Noch were used, which come already ground and with a brush for application. As with all weathering, rub the chalks in the direction that the weathering would naturally form.

To create spots of rust on a container, dab on a few drops of matt varnish where you want the rust to sit on the model.

Using two different shades of Noch weathering chalks, we dabbed chalk on the spots of still wet matt varnish and used the brush to rub up and down the container sides. Weathering with chalks can be a messy job, as can be seen here, so it is essential to use old newspaper under your work area.

To the left is a pristine container and to the right one that has some areas of rust added. The container to the right looks as if it might be nearing the end of its serviceable life.

This Bachmann container wagon was weathered by Danish modeller Pelle Søeborg using an airbrush (left and below). To find out more about Pelle's techniques see his **Done in a Day: Easy Detailing and Weathering Projects** *book with over 235 colour photographs. The various levels of weathering are particularly well illustrated. Other topics include the addition of graffiti to rolling stock and the ageing of containers.*

WEATHERING STARTER KITS

Various companies retail weathering kit packs including DoubleO Scenics, whose set contains twelve weathering powders, two brush applicators, one plastic mixing tray, three wagons bodies and instructions on how to use the set. Supplying the OO-scale wagon bodies on which to practise your techniques is a good way of gaining confidence before moving on to your rolling stock. The accompanying instructions are very good indeed.

Various companies offer to weather ready-to-run wagons and locomotives where the manufacturer does not offer the wagons ready-weathered.

Tips for Weathering

- Look at real trains to see how they age. Take your own photographs of them to refer to as you weather the models. Work from prototype pictures to see exactly how a particular wagon would weather over time. Look where the rust patches are likely to occur.
- Practise weathering on older models first. You may not mind having to lose these models if your first attempts at weathering turn out to be not as good as you would like. Bear in mind that many weathering effects can be erased, depending upon the materials used.
- Start lightly and gradually build up the weathering to avoid overdoing the effect. You can always add another layer of weathering.

- If you are really nervous about weathering, use materials that are reversible such as water-soluble weathering dyes or weathering powders that can be rubbed off. Use the materials that you are most comfortable with.
- Type 'weathering wagons' (or something similar) into any Internet search engine and a multitude of tips will soon be found. Read magazine articles and books on weathering and watch the DVDs that are available.
- When you are happy with the finished result, the weathering can be sealed in and protected by a quick spray of matt varnish from an aerosol. This usually has the effect of toning down the weathering.

CHAPTER ELEVEN

MODERN SCENIC PRODUCTS AND TECHNIQUES

Never has it been easier to make great-looking scenery.

Making scenery has never been so enjoyable. There is a huge array of products from which to create great-looking scenics. Ranging from laser-cut plants through to trees that actually look like trees, our scenery can be made to look very realistic.

WHAT MODERN PRODUCTS ARE AVAILABLE?

Following is a summary of the products that are now available for scenic modellers.

Tufts of grass Clumps, tufts and strips of grass in a number of colours are available from various manufacturers. Some are plain grass, others include various coloured foam pieces to represent flowers.

These can easily be fixed to the layout with a dab of PVA adhesive.

Good-quality grass mats Many of us remember those bright green grass mats from European scenic manufacturers. Things have certainly come a long way since then, because grass mats are now available with vari-levelled fibres, multicoloured grasses and earth effects. Some of the major scenic manufacturers, including Heki and Noch, even retail mats of static grass fibres planted in an invisible mesh ready to be added to layouts.

Static grass During the last few years, static grass fibres have become increasingly popular, offering a carpet-tuft appearance to the landscape rather than

A weathered Heljan Class 26 locomotive passes through scenery intended to represent Scotland. Various layers of static grass fibres have been planted. The fence was made from florist's wire and elastic thread, the back is a photo scene and the Scots pine tree is by 4D Model Shop.

One of the more recent scenic products available is packs of laser-cut card plants.

Looking across this valley, the trees make a good backdrop to the Jinty tank. Most of the trees in this scene were made from kits and the ready-made ones were improved by adding additional texture and colour variations.

the flatter appearance that comes from using traditional scatter materials. Recently, new tools have come on the market, plus new grass fibres for both the small (N and Z scales) and larger (O and above) scales. The cost of the more sophisticated applicators can be an issue, but while the inexpensive puffer bottle might not be good for planting lots of grass, it does make static grass a scenic possibility for all. There are also electrostatic grass applicators available at less than £30.

Trees and hedges Bottle-brush trees and plastic trunks with blobs of lichen on the top are far removed from the quality models of trees that are available today. The latest trees are either ready to plant or basic trees that can easily be improved. In addition, there are many good tree kits.

Plants In both plastic and laser-cut thin card there are now lots of tiny plants available in scales ranging from Z through to O. Careful use of these plants, plus some toning down of the colours, is a good way to feature detailed plants in the foreground scenes on layouts.

Water One-step ready-mixed fluids make the task of adding a water feature to a layout easy and fun. Just remember to follow the instructions carefully and allow the recommended drying time and depth of water for successful results.

Wallpaper rollers have several uses when making scenery, including positioning a back scene on the plywood (or other) timber support for the back scene and working with brick papers and pavement papers.

Hedgerow Scenics retails superb hedges such as these. The use of real wood pieces, good colour and fine foliage and leaves makes them irresistible to add to a suitable layout.

Water adds life to a layout. This waterfall was made by 'hanging' strips of dried Woodland Scenics Water Effects over a cliff.

In the following sections, we will look at the various ways of adding grass and trees to your layout.

WHAT IS AVAILABLE TO MAKE GRASS?

Does real grass all look the same? The quick answer is no. Grass is not always just found in back gardens – it is everywhere. Grass is not always short and it is not always green. The texture of grass varies enormously. Some grass is plain, some has flowers, some has seeds, some is rough. The texture of grass is generally uneven, other than on newly mown gardens and sports fields.

The colour of grass changes with the seasons. In winter it might look a trampled-down brown/green colour, whilst in spring it takes on a vivid green appearance. The height of wild grass changes with the seasons. It may look very flat in winter compared to when it is at its tallest in late summer.

There is plenty of choice of scenic materials on the market today to represent the great variety of grass and ground cover.

Sawdust-based scatter material This long-established method is probably the cheapest way of covering the ground, although it has the disadvantage

of looking flat on the landscape. The material can be obtained in numerous colours.

Clumps, tufts and strips of grasses These can be obtained in a numerous colours. Some are plain grass in seasonal colours, whilen others represent flowers.

Grass mats Good-quality grass mats are available these days, as well as 'static grass on a roll'.

Static grass When fixed to the landscape using specific tools, static grass fibres give a 3D effect that is becoming increasingly popular among modellers.

Finely chopped pieces of foam These are available in very fine, fine, medium and coarse. The range of colours is large, as is the number of firms making these products. Mixed scatter materials for specific seasons and locations such as a heather mixture, spring flower mixture, moorland mixture and forest floor are also available.

Other materials Teddy bear fur can be teased out to represent tall grass. Hanging basket liner is a good way to reproduce tall, random grasses. Rubberized horsehair is suitable for ragged patches of tall weeds and grasses.

In BR Blue days, a Class 03 locomotive by Bachmann hauls a short china clay train. The vegetation was made mainly from rubberized horsehair. The track is Code 75 ballasted with very fine sand.

Three layers of static grass fibres were planted on this O-scale lineside scene layout built by John Emerson. Extra-hold hairspray was then 'wafted' over the grass fibres and bits of red foam were sprinkled on to represent red poppies.

Below, we will look in detail at how to work with grass tufts, strips and mats and how to apply static grass.

WORKING WITH GRASS TUFTS AND STRIPS

Most railway depots, stations and lineside areas are strewn with tall grasses and weeds. Road sides and industrial areas are often full of grasses and weeds too. The colours will vary with the seasons; for example, the grasses in early summer will be deeper green than in late summer, when they will be tinged with yellow and brown.

Grass tufts and strips are available from Gaugemaster, Heki, miniNatur, Model Tree Shop, Noch, Train Terrain and Treemendus. The grass tufts can be removed from their backing sheet and used singly or in multiples. They are sold in seasonal colours and suitablility for smaller or larger scales. Some feature tiny leaf effects. Cutting the tufts and strips with scissors gives you smaller dots of grass tufts, which can be especially useful in the smaller scales.

Grass tufts and clumps are simply dots of tall grass. Tufts can be removed from their packaging with tweezers and then a spot of adhesive dabbed on to their base to fix them to the landscape. Some come with adhesive on the base, but it is always worth setting them in a small blob of PVA adhesive

or contact adhesive. These can be positioned on the layout singly or along with several others. Mix some of the coloured clumps together in a garden setting to provide a summer border.

Grass strips are sold in various thicknesses and colours. They are useful for along the edge of a ploughed field, or as the central grass strip in a farm track. Again, they can be stuck to the baseboard with PVA or contact adhesive.

If you want to add further variety to your grass, this is easy to do by running a brush that has been dipped in PVA along the top of the grass. Then sprinkle on different-coloured best-quality fine foam scatter material. The glue will dry clear.

CHOOSING AND USING GRASS MATS

Many grass mats are ready planted with static grass and some of today's better mats are very realistic. These mats enable a time-starved modeller to cover areas of ground quickly and realistically. The latest mats contain grasses of different heights and colours, though it must be added that the best mats are quite expensive to buy. The most realistic high-quality grass mats around at the moment are by Busch, Faller, Hedgerow Scenics, Heki, Langmesser Modellwelt, miniNatur, Model Scene of the Czech Republic and Noch. The miniNatur range of mats offers especially good grass mats for the larger scales in addition to those for OO/HO.

Grass mats cover large areas quickly and 'solidly'. Nowhere does the colour of the base material show through. The more expensive grass mats can be laid on their own and do not generally require additional layers of scenic detailing.

It is best not to lay these mats as they come. Pull them apart gently, make random pieces and push them into brushed-on adhesive. By teasing the mats apart, they will cover a larger area. Pull off the backing sheet before you pull apart the mat. Push the torn-off sections of grass mat into wet glue.

Grass mats are now available with fibres of different colours, textures and heights. Some include sand, pieces of timber and other details. These mats are not intended just to be positioned whole on the layout, but should be used in smaller pieces like a jigsaw puzzle.

One corner of a good-quality grass mat showing coloured plants embedded in the mat. These plants could be carefully torn or cut from the mat one by one and used to represent daffodils on a layout.

The Busch range of good-quality grass mats is large and here we show just three pieces, with a 1p coin for size-comparison purposes.

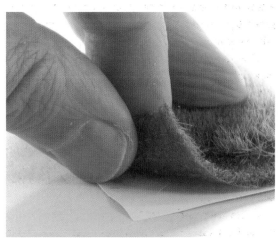

Teasing the grass mat from its backing sheet is easy between your fingers. Whilst some grass mats are self-adhesive, I always use PVA adhesive or similar to fix them to the landscape to be doubly sure that they stay in place.

Never be tempted to use the grass mat sheets as they come. Tear them off in random-sized pieces and then use them on the layout in a jigsaw manner. The result will be more realistic.

A selection of random pieces of grass mat ready to be placed in adhesive on the landscape. These pieces are only 10 or 12mm (½in) across.

Rather than cover all the adhesive, this shows some pieces of grass mat already positioned in adhesive. The gaps between the pieces of grass mat will be covered in real sand, fine foam scatter material and various plants.

Close up of a finished part of a diorama showing the grass mat pieces, sand and plastic flowers by Busch.

Another view of the completed diorama intended to be sandy dunes in a coastal location. Alternatively, it could be a sandy forest floor.

HOW TO USE THE CHEAPER GRASS MATS

A grass mat can simply be laid on top of brushed PVA adhesive but they can look rather crumpled if they are not cut into smaller pieces which are much easier to work with one at a time. Once the PVA has dried under a cheaper grass mat detailing can be done by brushing on PVA adhesive then sprinkling on some fine and coarse scatter material in various places. Later brush on more PVA adhesive then plant static grasses from various suppliers applied with a Noch Gras Master or puffer bottle. Tease out pieces of foliage from Heki (Heki Flor) and Woodlands Scenics (Foliage mats) and others then push the sections into spread PVA to represent low ground cover and weeds. Grass tufts, clumps of foam and taller grasses can then be 'planted' into blobs of PVA.

HOW TO USE STATIC GRASS ON A ROLL

Prolific German scenery manufacturers Heki and Noch retail what is effectively 'static grass on a roll':

Heki Realistic Wildgras This is sold in four colours with 6mm ($\frac{1}{4}$in) tall grass fibres on an almost invisible mesh net. Each piece is around 450 x 170mm (17$\frac{1}{4}$ x 6$\frac{3}{4}$in), but because it is best 'teased out' it can cover an area almost twice that size.

Heki Kreative Wildgras This is retailed in four shades of green. It comes in the same size as Realistic Wildgras, but is more suitable for cutting with scissors and randomly positioning on the landscape.

Gaugemaster and Noch Natur + Meadow Mats These are a good way to add 12mm ($\frac{1}{2}$in) tall static grass if you do not have a an electrostatic grass tool. The mats can be torn or cut and then glued on to the landscape. Various colours are available.

These mats can be planted whole or in pieces. It is very easy to break off pieces of the mat between your fingers, or alternatively scissors or a craft knife can be used to cut off pieces of the mat. Push and slide them together on top of spread PVA or scenic glue. Butt up the pieces closely to give a seamless effect. The mats easily follow the contours of any landscape. It is not always necessary to paint the landscape before laying the mats because of the density of the grass fibres.

STATIC GRASS

The use of static grass on model railway layouts in the UK is becoming increasingly popular. Modellers love the 3D effect that is possible by using static grass. The results are generally much more realistic than a flat landscape texture created by using traditional scatter materials. It is easy to plant good-looking static grass and in the past couple of years many more tools and grass fibres have come on to the market that are now suitable for Z through to O scales and above. There has never been a better time to enter the world of static grass.

WHAT IS STATIC GRASS?

Static grass is made from very fine polyfibre lengths and is retailed in various lengths and colours. When fixed to the landscape using specific tools the fibres give a carpet-tuft effect, with the fibres standing upright in the ground. Static grass is also known as electrostatic grass because of the process involved in planting it.

Static grass is dependent upon a tiny electrical charge that the grass fibres pick up in the dispensing tool. They retain this charge as they fly through the air and stick to the adhesive that has been brushed on to the landscape. When the glue is dry, the tiny strands of imitation grass are left standing in a vertical position in the landscape.

With electrostatic devices, a connection is made between the tool (by way of a wire and an alligator clip) and the land just before the grass is to be planted. The alligator clip needs to be attached to the nearest section of rail, or a nail or a pin inserted into the baseboard near to the area to be treated. This creates the electrical circuit to ensure that the grass particles land in an upright position in the glue on the landscape. With the plastic puffer bottles, the electrostatic charge comes from the shaking of the fibres in the bottle.

Some modellers use static grass extensively, whilst others keep it for specific areas on their layouts. There is no right or wrong way to use static grass, though once a modeller has experimented with it there is an almost 100 per cent guarantee that he will want to use it a lot more in the future.

STATIC GRASS FIBRES

Static grass fibres are made by an increasing number of companies, including Anita Decor, Busch, DCC Train Automation, DoubleO Scenics, Faller, Green Scene, Heki, Javis, miniNatur, Noch, Woodland Scenics and WW Scenics.

Grass fibres vary in both length and colour, ranging from 1mm through to 12mm, and come in a large selection of colour shades. Because of this variety, multiple levels of grass can be modelled and every season can be represented realistically. The grasses can be used to suit different locations, for example shorter grasses in a garden setting, longer at the trackside. Short grass might only need one application, but longer grasses may require several layers of static grass to build up the height of grass.

Multiple layers of static grass make the lineside appearance of this riverside diorama look more visually appealing compared to using simply green scatter material.

CLOCKWISE FROM TOP LEFT:

One of the more recent electrostatic grass-fibre tools is by WW Scenics. It comes with three different-sized mesh screw-on tops so that it can successfully plant grass fibres from 1–12mm. Such tools retail at around £100.

For less than £5, a plastic puffer bottle is a good way to plant small areas of static grass fibres. These are available from Gaugemaster, Noch, WW Scenics and others.

There are lots of manufacturers now retailing static grass fibres. The colour range is now vast, with some packs available in ready-mixed seasonal tints.

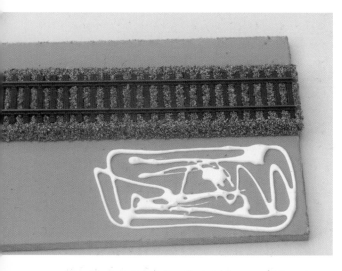

The first step to planting static grass fibres is to pour some adhesive on to the landscape. PVA is suitable for this, or one of the specialist scenic glues.

Spread the adhesive evenly with a wide paintbrush so that the entire area is covered. Limit yourself to working with 100sq cm at a time to ensure that the adhesive will still be wet when you plant the grass fibres.

The alligator clip on the electrostatic tool needs to be attached to the landscape in some way. This can be to the rail of track adjacent to the area to be planted, or to a pin knocked into the surface of the landscape.

Close-up of the effect that static grass fibres can give. This looks a lot more realistic than just scatter material.

IS STATIC GRASS JUST AN EXPENSIVE TECHNIQUE?

Definitely not. Whilst some of the electrostatic tools cost more than £100, there are many cheaper alternatives. Just some of the ways to keep the costs down include: Gaugemaster has a Static Grass Starter Set, which includes a puffer bottle, a bag of 2.5mm light green static grass plus a small plastic bottle of adhesive, and costs less than £10 and is a good way to experiment with static grass; Finescale Model World and DoubleO Scenics retail electrostatic grass tools at around £30 (www.finescalemodelworld.co.uk and www.doubleOscenics.co.uk); bags of static grass fibres cost from around £1.50 upwards and special glue is not required, as PVA glue works very well with all the popular grass fibres.

STATIC GRASS TOOLS AND MATERIALS

There are two main types of static grass tools: electrostatic devices that require battery or mains power and which retail between £28 and £180; and plastic puffer bottles that are available from less that £5. In addition, industrial static grass applicator tools are available at around £900. If the price of some of these electronic tools seems expensive, a model railway club could buy one and hire it out to members in the same way it does with reference books. Or a couple of friends with scenic layouts might decide to buy one jointly.

There are many homemade alternatives to these tools, including balloons, vacuum cleaners and other contraptions. These work with varying degrees of success and if you search the various model railway forums, you will find information on how to make these. A word of warning – be careful when using mains electricity with any of these devices.

Following is an overview of the tools and materials:

- Acrylic or emulsion paint to cover the landscape before applying the static grass. An aerosol of acrylic paint is a quick way to do this.
- An electrostatic grass tool or puffer bottle.
- PVA or any of the more specialized scenic adhesives. Extra-hold unscented hairspray is an alternative to PVA for the second and third layers of grass.

- A selection of static grass fibres. Fine foam scatter materials of different colours and textures from Busch, DoubleO, Noch, Treemendus, Woodland Scenics, WW Scenics and so on add variety of texture to finished static grass.
- Wide flat paintbrushes for painting the landscape with paint and then the glue once the paint has dried.
- When working with the longest grass fibres, a vacuum cleaner can be used to raise up the fibres as the glue sets. A vacuum should also be used suck up any excess fibres before you begin running trains again.

PREPARING THE GROUND

As when using scatter material, it is necessary to paint the landscape fully in a subdued colour such as brown or green (acrylic or emulsion paint are ideal) before treating it with static grass. This is because the static grass fibres will stand upright and the base colour of the scenery might be visible when looking from above through the upright fibres.

A really quick way of painting white plaster cloth once it has dried is to use acrylic aerosols. Primer aerosols from car shops are another good source of suitable paint.

A shortcut is to use glue that is already coloured, then apply the scenic materials directly into the glue. Faller, Heki and WW Scenics retail a selection of coloured glues, but what is to stop us adding brown or green paint to PVA adhesive? Just experiment with a small amount of your chosen paint to ensure that it mixes well.

PLANTING STATIC GRASS WITH AN ELECTROSTATIC TOOL

It is very easy to plant static grass. Many of the techniques are common to the more usual scenic processes and once you have learned the basic principles you will be able to experiment with the multiple uses of electrostatic grass on dioramas and layouts.

For tools with screw-on meshes, the fine mesh sieve is best suited to the short grass fibres, whilst the larger mesh sieves are best for the longer grass fibres. Half fill up the grass applicator device with your chosen static grasses. It is advisable to do this before you paint on the glue because you need to work quite quickly after the glue is painted on to the landscape. To fix the static grass fibres to the landscape you can use PVA adhesive, though some scenic manufacturers do retail their own products for this purpose. Use a wide paintbrush to spread the PVA on to the landscape and ensure that all of the area to be treated is covered in glue, because fibres will only stick where there is glue. I find that to get the best results it is advisable to limit work on applying static grass to areas of about 100sq cm (15.5sq in) at a time.

Attach the metal alligator clip of the electronic device to a rail of a section of track near to the area that you want to work on. If the area is remote from the track, knock a pin or nail into the landscape and attach the alligator clip to the pin. I find that Woodland Scenics Foam Nails (also known a T-pins) are ideal for this purpose. This connection with the layout is necessary to provide the electrostatic link between the charge in the grass tool and the ground.

Switch on the electronic grass tool, invert it and gently shake it from side to side about 7mm (¼in) over the surface of the glue and watch the grasses fall into the glue in an upright position. Once you have treated the area covered with the glue with the static grass, switch off the tool and leave the area to dry.

Not all static grass fibres will stick to the glue the first time. If your layout is portable after the glue has dried, shake off the excess grass fibres and save them for use again. If the layout is not portable, use a soft 2in (50mm) paintbrush to sweep the excess grass fibres into piles to collect them for reuse later.

PLANTING FIBRES WITH A PUFFER BOTTLE

The Gaugemaster, Noch and WW Scenics Puffer Bottles of course have no 'electronic link'– it is the action of 'puffing up' the grass fibres in the plastic bottle that provides the necessary electrostatic charge to the fibres.

Using a puffer bottle is easy: first paint the baseboard a solid colour using acrylics or similar. Leave to dry. Choose the colours and lengths of static grass that you wish to use on the landscape and unscrew the top of the bottle and take out the plug with the holes in. Pour in the chosen mixture of static grass fibres to about half way and push home the plug.

Brush glue on to the ready-painted surface of the landscape and while the glue is still tacky pump up the plastic bottle in your hands several times. Tip the bottle upside down so that the plug end of the bottle is about 60–80mm (2.4–3.2in) above the area to be treated, then squeeze the sides of the puffer bottle as quickly as you can a few times so that the grasses 'shoot' out of the bottle on to the sticky adhesive. Move the bottle along to cover the area that has been spread with glue and leave the treated section to dry.

If your layout calls for tall grass or weeds, repeat the process a second or third time over the whole or parts of the area to be treated.

TAKING IT TO THE NEXT LEVEL

When the basics of planting static grass have been mastered, there are various advanced techniques that can be used. These include creating:

- Very tall grass.
- Natural-looking colour variations.
- Multiple levels of grasses and colours.

CREATING TALL GRASS

You may be content with the first layer of static grass, or you may wish that all or some of the treated areas could be taller grass. Wait until the adhesive has fully dried on the first layer of grass, then thinly brush on a second layer of PVA with a wide paintbrush over some or all of the surface of the already planted static grass. Then pass the electronic tool over the surface again, but with slightly different colour variations of grasses to the first application. Again, leave to dry.

Another alternative to using PVA glue where you want a lighter covering of secondary static grass is to spray some extra-hold unscented hairspray over the area to be treated. Whilst hairspray cannot be applied in such a controlled manner as brushed-on PVA, it is useful for a light spread of adhesive to 'catch' random fibres.

CREATING NATURAL-LOOKING COLOUR VARIATIONS

Use acrylic spray paints or an airbrush to add further colours very sparingly to your landscapes. Or you could try lightly brush-painting the fibres. For example, where you would like tall summer bleached grass along the roadside or trackside, use a little straw-coloured acrylic paint on a brush to pass lightly through the grass fibres. You will be surprised at how quickly this method changes the appearance of your scenery.

MULTIPLE-LEVEL GRASSES AND COLOURS

Go outside and observe some tall grasses. The lower strands will usually be greener than the top strands of grass. To replicate this effect, lay a first layer of shortest grass (say, 1.5mm or 4mm on an OO-scale layout), then leave to dry. Later, use a brush or pipette to add drops or areas of white glue. Then add a layer of lighter-colour 6mm grass fibres. Once the excess grass fibres have been blown off you will see the multiple-level effect of the grass fibres.

Dry-brushing planted grass fibres is a good way of adding colour variation. Just drag a paintbrush across the tops of the fibres.

To make small tufts of grass add drops of adhesive to the landscape, then plant grass with an electrostatic tool or puffer bottle. The second tier of fibres will only stick to the wet adhesive, so you can build up clumps of patchy grass and weeds.

This section of landscape uses multiple layers of static grass fibres of different colours and lengths. It is fun to add the extra layers of grass fibres and visually they make the scene much more interesting.

MAKING A FIELD OF POPPIES

To add variations in colour and texture to the planted static grasses, spray a little hairspray over some areas, then sprinkle on some fine foam and/or coarse scatters. This is an easy way of adding a 'dash of colour' to the landscape. For example, to create a poppy field or a patch of poppies sprinkle some tiny pieces of red foam scatter through your fingers on top of just-applied hairspray. Then seal the poppy flowers to the landscape with another light coating of the hairspray. If some have planted themselves where you did not want them, it is simple to remove the flower heads by using a small pair of tweezers to pluck them off the grass.

By combining traditional materials such as rubberized horsehair with the more modern materials such as static grass fibres, the scenic modeller can achieve the 'best of both worlds'.

Tips for Planting Static Grass

- First, paint the baseboard a solid colour using acrylic, latex, emulsion paints or similar. This is necessary to prevent the colour of the baseboard showing between the static grass fibres as one looks down through the planted grass fibres. Leave the paint to dry before adding the adhesive and the grass fibres.
- Choose the colours and lengths of static grass that you wish to use on the landscape. The longest fibres will be necessary for the larger scales.
- Do not be tempted to use the brightest grass fibres. The more subdued the colour, the more realistic it will look. Be careful not to mix seasonal colours.
- Spread the adhesive on the landscape with a wide, flat paintbrush in areas of about 100sq cm (15.5sq in) at a time. If the area is any larger, the adhesive will start to dry out before the fibres have been planted. With the adhesive still wet, use the tool to apply static grass fibres.
- Leave the planted section to dry. The length of drying time of the adhesive will depend upon the time of year and the location in which you are doing the work. The warmer the room, the quicker it will dry.
- Only after you are convinced that the static grass fibres are firmly fixed down on the baseboard should you shake or vacuum off any excess static grasses that have not stuck to the adhesive. Reuse the unused static grass fibres if possible.
- If your layout calls for tall grass or weeds repeat the process a second or third time over the whole or parts of the area to be treated. Just keep on painting adhesive on to planted grass fibres, then add more fibres to build up the height of the grass.
- If you want to just plant a few areas of taller grass try spraying extra-hold hairspray in the area of already planted grass. It acts as a good adhesive for static grass fibres.
- To add additional texture variations run a paintbrush partly loaded with adhesive over the top of planted grass fibres, then sprinkle on various fine foam scatter materials of the appropriate size and colours. This creates the illusion of flower and weed heads.
- When using the 10 and 12mm grass lengths it is necessary to run a vacuum cleaner over the surface of the newly planted grasses a few minutes after they have been planted into the glue. In this way they will stand upright and not simply fall back down into the adhesive.

Static Grass Fibres – Which Lengths Can be Used for Which Scale?

Length/scale	Z	N	OO	O
1mm	Yes	Yes	No	No
1.5mm	Yes	Yes	Yes	No
2.5mm	Yes	Yes	Yes	No
4mm	No	No	Yes	Yes
6mm	No	No	Yes	Yes
10mm	No	No	Yes	Yes
12mm	No	No	No	Yes

TREES

Today's scenic modellers are blessed with a good selection of models of trees in various scales. The trees come in highly detailed form or as basic trees either as deciduous or coniferous trees.

WHAT MODERN PRODUCTS ARE AVAILABLE?

Ready-made models of trees have come a very long way in the last decade. Today, the scenic modeller is spoilt for choice. Many ready-assembled trees look good straight out of the packaging. Others require a little work to improve their appearance, but definitely have the potential of becoming a realistic-looking tree compared to some models of trees that require a substantial amount of work to make them acceptable to the modeller's eye. In addition, there are many tree components available right down to miniature leaves and a number of tree kits that feature a variety of materials, such as wire, tree armatures, plastic trunks, white metal trunks – the list goes on. There are a number of companies that offer a bespoke tree-making service.

READY-TO-PLANT TREES

A few years ago, companies just offered models of either coniferous or deciduous trees. Things are very different now. Today, modellers want model trees that look like trees – of the correct species, for the correct season and of the correct height. There are an increasing number of model tree manufacturers. Some are big-name manufacturers, whilst others are scenic specialists. Some of the larger manufacturers tend to offer ranges of trees, including economy packs of a number of basic trees, standard-quality trees and premium-quality trees. Usually, the higher the price tag on a tree, the better the model.

Many of the trees made by mainstream model railway companies are now of good quality. These manufacturers include Anita Decor, Bachmann Scenescapes, Busch, Faller, Gaugemaster, Heki, Hornby Skale Scenics, K & M, Noch, The Model Tree Shop, Viessmann and Woodland Scenics. Some firms such as Faller, Gaugemaster, Heki, Hornby Skale Scenics, Noch and Woodland Scenics retail bumper bags of trees that usually represent good value. The tree shapes are typical rather than detailed and as such these are useful trees for the background scenes on layouts.

Anita Decor manufactures trees that are beautifully crafted using natural components. Being handmade, they are suitable as specimen trees at the front of layouts. The company retail trees that suit various scales, for example oak trees in heights of 25, 35 and 45cm.

Some companies specialize in architectural model trees (for example, 4D Model Shop and Treemendus) and these are generally of a very good standard. Manufacturers of architectural tree models also offer a bespoke tree-building service if a specific size, shape and kind of tree is required. These are ideal for single standing specimen trees and those near to the viewing edge of a layout, where the budget permits it.

Many of the European manufacturers retail fruit trees complete with miniature fruit. Whilst some of these are realistic, others feature fruit that may be intended to look like apples, but in scale terms look more the size of pumpkins!

One useful source of trees is The Model Tree Shop (www.themodeltreeshop.co.uk), which sells tree ranges made in three methods: string and wire; etched brass; and twisted wire. Take a look at their website – the number of model trees that this company retails is amazing.

MAKING TREES FROM WIRE

Wire suitable for trees can be purchased from florist shops or specialist model suppliers. It is either sold on a reel or in lengths. Firstly, decide what height the tree will be, which will determine the longest length of wire that will be needed to form the basis of the trunk for the tree. The lengths of wire can be cut as necessary with wire cutters that are obtainable from any DIY stores.

Secondly, study the shape of the real tree that you intend to model. The correct tree profile can

One lone well-made tree makes a real contribution to any layout. This tree is made from wire by 4D Model Shop.

This stand of mixed trees at Pendon is mainly made from wound wire and foliage material. Pendon Museum has so many trees on its layouts that it sets up a production line to make them.

be found in one of the many books about trees that are available. Keep the book close by as you make the tree and refer to it from time to time to ensure that your model looks authentic. How many main branches does a typical tree have? Does it have a close-knit branch structure, or are the branches few in number? Is the trunk very thick or slender? The answers to these questions will determine the number of lengths of wire that will be needed for each particular tree. Basically, the more branches and the thicker the trunk, the more lengths of wire that will need to be wound.

To start making a tree, take the longest lengths of wire and twist them around each other one by one. For the length of the main trunk, all the wires will need to be wound around each other tightly for the lower section of the tree to form the trunk, leaving the top two-thirds of the wires generally untwisted. Twisting wire is not a task that you can do for hours on end. It is rather wearisome on the fingers and you may find that it is best to limit the time spent on the task. Once you are happy with the shape of the main trunk, you can begin to twist the wires to form the main branches. When you have twisted the number of main branches, stand back and look at the shape of the tree. Does it compare well with the tree profile that you are aiming to achieve? Use finer-diameter wire to add further branches.

There are several ways of adding the bark. Some modellers wrap the main trunk and the main branches with florist's tape, to be followed by adding tree bark material. Others simply add tree bark material to the trunk and branches. Tree bark can be one of three different materials:

- Flexible sealant obtainable from DIY stores; ideally this should be dark grey or brown in colour, but if not mix in a little paint to colour it.
- Tree bark powder that needs to be mixed with PVA adhesive – this is obtainable from Treemendus and other suppliers.
- Ready-mixed tree bark obtainable from Green Scene and International Models.

Whichever method you use, the tree bark material can be brushed on to the trunk and main branches

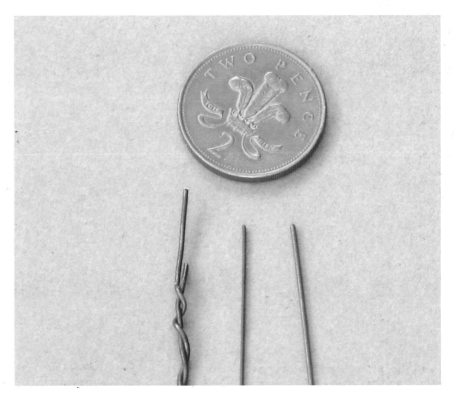

This selection of wire was bought from a florist's shop and specialist suppliers at model railway shows.

Two Pendon wire willow trees under construction. Note the bark effect; one is already painted. The trees stand in a wooden block during the construction process.

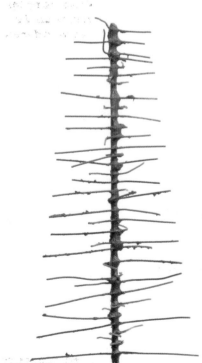

A handmade conifer tree armature made by winding wire and then gluing the wires together with a hot glue gun.

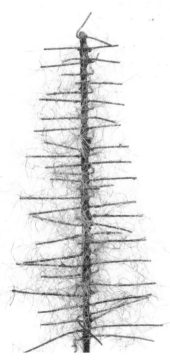

The same tree armature now has added grass fibres to build up the foliage in layers. The more layers of fibres that are added, the denser the foliage will become.

By using static grass fibres and miniNatur foliage, this wire tree armature has been transformed into a realistic-looking tree as made by Stephan Kraus.

Close-up of the foliage on the completed tree.

A deciduous tree using wire for its trunk and branches with light foliage at Pendon Museum.

using an old flat paintbrush. It is not necessary to get a perfectly smooth finish – tree bark is never that! Leave the tree bark to dry for at least twenty-four hours. Go back to your book of trees and see what the colour of the bark is on the actual tree. Acrylic paints can be used to colour the trunk and main branches using a paintbrush or acrylic aerosol spray paints, or by using an airbrush.

Tree trunks are rarely one colour, so it will be worth highlighting various parts of the trunk with different-colour paints by dry brushing. Once the paint is dry on the trunk and the branches, it is time to add the foliage. Again, study the reference book to see if the foliage is dense or light and airy. This may depend upon the season that you are modelling.

There are various materials available for tree foliage from Heki, miniNatur or Woodland Scenics, for example foliage mats and sections that can be cut and teased out from the main piece to form 'clumps' of foliage. Woodland Scenics Poly Fibre is a light and airy material that can be teased out from the main ball. Treemendus canopy is fine twisted pastiche material that can easily be teased out from its twine. Rubberized horsehair can be sprayed green and teased out to form foliage and finally sea moss pieces create a light and airy foliage effect.

These materials can be prepared appropriately according to the size of tree. Do not attempt to cover a tree with one piece of teased-out foliage – it is generally much better to use more, smaller pieces. The foliage pieces can be fixed to the branches using dabs of PVA adhesive or contact adhesive, which then needs to be left to dry.

Add some individual leaves to the tree. There are various excellent products for this process, including Noch Laub (leaves) and any of the fine scatters now available. Use a couple of quick bursts of supermarket extra-hold unscented hairspray across the foliage, then by hand sprinkle on the leaf material. Do not apply so much leaf material as to cover the foliage. The intention is to add texture and variety to the foliage. When you are content that the tree is as good as it can be, spray it either with more hairspray or with Woodland Scenics Scenic Cement, or any

other designated scenic glue from Treemendus or Deluxe Materials.

If making a tree in winter it is not necessary to add leaves and foliage. A tree outline could be sprayed grey. Adding sea moss to the branches they spraying the entire tree grey can create a convincing deciduous tree in winter. Plant the tree in the landscape and fix with a blob of PVA adhesive.

This tree armature was purchased from miniNatur and comes complete with coloured bark effect.

Next step was to cut up pieces of miniNatur foliage with scissors to be added to the armature. The foliage can be teased out too.

Between my fingers I manipulated the 'wire branches' so that they pointed in all directions.

Close-up of the drooping foliage on a branch. The foliage was fixed using Busch scenic glue.

This is the completed tree after about two hours' work.

A conifer tree made from balsa wood, shaped with a sharp craft knife. Florist's wire was pushed through holes in the trunk and bent over, then foliage added from a foliage mat.

To the left and the right are trees made from Heki plastic tree armatures. To the left the tree is lightly covered in foliage mat, but the tree to the right uses lots of teased-out poly-fibre to give a denser foliage. The tree in the middle was made from a weathered spruce kit by miniNatur.

This rural scene is partially completed. The retaining wall is by Heki. It has just one coat of paint and the first layer of scenic materials.

The same scene, but now the wall has been dry-brushed a darker colour to make the stonework more obvious and various creeping plants, made from Woodland Scenics Poly Fibre treated with scatter materials, now grow up the wall. The scene looks much more complete than the previous picture.

Tree armatures form the trunk and branches of a tree. We are very familiar with armatures moulded in plastic from companies such as Woodland Scenics but these are also available made from wire with the trunk and main parts of the branches coated in a flexible material which comes ready painted. The range by Langmesser Modellwelt includes both deciduous and conifers and is suitable for scales N upwards. A tree armature such as these would probably taken up to 2 to 3 hours to make to this standard. The branches on the armatures need to be twisted around through the fingers but this is just a five minute job.

INTERLUDE ON THE WISBECH AND UPWELL

Even a small layout can endeavour to capture the flavour of a well-known line. Here we have a glimpse of the Wisbech and Upwell Tramway using all 'off the peg' equipment. The line running alongside a road was one of the memorable features of the now-closed line. This layout was built for British Railway Modelling (BRM) magazine.

The row of cottages on the Wisbech layout were Hornby Skaledale models with repainted front doors, curtains, different stages of weathering, a pavement using Metcalfe paving slabs and various figures and road vehicles.

Class 04 11102 is shunting in the yard. The basis for this locomotive used a Bachmann Trains USA locomotive that I imported into the UK. There is more road traffic to be seen on the layout than there would have been in real life at the time.

In reality, lorries caused the demise of this line, so here we have two of the line's opposition racing the train towards the cottages.

The tram locomotive used a Bachmann Trains USA 'Toby' locomotive as its basis. I added various details to give an overall impression of the famous tram locomotive.

Well-used fruit vans and a coal wagon would have been seen frequently on the real Wisbech railway line.

At some places along the line I planted static grass fibres between the rails to create the illusion that the line was infrequently used.

CHAPTER TWELVE

ADDING THE DETAILS

The details are what most people notice first on a layout.

The scenic accessory aspect is one of the fastest growing sectors of the hobby. There are many small firms that make a valuable contribution to the hobby, in addition to the larger well-known names.

FIGURES

Adding figures and small scenes to a layout creates points of interest for the viewer. If your layout is small, such cameo scenes might even distract from the tiny size of the layout. Figures are available in all the common scales from numerous manufacturers in every imaginable pose. Some come ready-painted and just need attaching to the layout. These are mainly made from plastic, but others need to be painted –

these are made from either plastic or white metal. Companies that make model figures include Aidan Campbell, Bachmann Scenecraft, Dapol, Dart Castings, Faller, Hornby, Kibri, Langley Models, Merten, Mike Pett, Model Scene, Montys, P & D Marsh, Preiser, Noch, Ten Commandments, Vollmer and Woodland Scenics.

Whilst many of these figures are OO scale, others from the European and American manufacturers are HO scale. Whilst some modellers insist on using only OO figures, other modellers are happy to use HO figures on OO-scale layouts provided that the two sizes of figures are not located next to each other.

The scope for detailing a layout with figures is enormous. For example, if you are modelling the Teignmouth sea wall in OO scale, Noch makes

A couple of pots with plants and a policewoman contribute to this cameo scene on a Shillingstone diorama. The building and the figure are by Bachmann Scenecraft, with the pots by Gaugemaster.

Ford station sign. Look out for these details as you travel around. Take photographs so that you can refer to them later.

Fences and more fences. Never before have modellers been so blessed in the main scales. The materials used include plastic and laser-cut timber.

Lineside signs are easy to make from the various cardboard sheets from Gaugemaster, Sankey Scenics and others. The posts are plastic rod. The speed restriction sign is a laser-cut sign from York Modelmaking.

HO-scale windsurfers, rowing and sailing boats, beach equipment, bathers, nude bathers (if you want those on your layout), bathers applying sun cream, anglers and so on. In addition to models of people, companies make miniature birds, animals, snakes, horses, dogs, cats, gulls, deer and many more.

Sadly, in most places we see rubbish in real life. Modelling such rubbish is an easy task once you find some bits and pieces.

Bits and bobs alongside this locomotive depot building were found in my spares box. I knew they would come in useful one day. They were fixed to the scene with spots of PVA.

Noch produces HO-scale figures of UK station personnel in the post-war era.

Figures for O scale can generally look splendid if they are painted nicely.

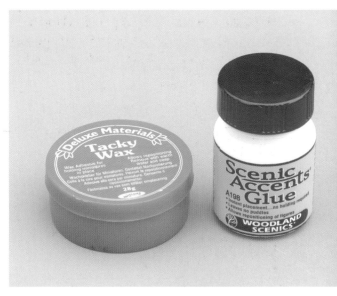

These two adhesives are very good for working with figures on a layout. The Tacky Wax is useful if you just want to position figures or accessories on a temporary basis, such as for a photographic shoot.

At Pendon Museum the figures are very well painted and are arranged to tell a story. This one is looking at his pocket watch – maybe the train is late?

It is approaching rush hour at this city station in the days of Network South East. Good-quality ready-painted figures are now readily available from Bachmann Scenecraft, Noch, Preiser and others.

These figures convey the impression of movement. Some European figures do actually move, with men chopping wood, young people dancing and many more. MODELLED AND PHOTOGRAPHED BY STEPHEN KRAUS

WORKING WITH FIGURES

Position the figures in groups or engaging in work. Do not be tempted to overpopulate a layout. Use small cameo scenes to increase the viewing interest of your layout. The layouts at Pendon Museum feature a lot of scenes with figures in natural poses such as chatting together. To fix the figures down use PVA, contact adhesive, Deluxe Materials Speed Bond, Hob-e-Tac or any of the other glues that are suitable. If you only wish to position the figures for a photograph, one of the repositionable glues such as Deluxe Materials Tacky Glue is ideal.

Even ready-painted figures can be improved by highlighting further details. A thin wash of black acrylic paint or weathering dye on finished figures removes the glossy appearance of ready-painted figures and will also highlight some of the details.

Unpainted metal figures should be cleaned with soap and water and when dry sprayed with a light coat of primer (for example, Halfords grey cellulose primer for cars). Use a 'base colour' for the whole figure as the colour that will cover the largest area.

Paint the figure with an airbrush or brush, using oil-or cellulose-based paints such as Humbrol. Allow the figure to dry fully, then paint on the details using acrylic paint. Always wash your hands carefully after working, cleaning or polishing white metal and use a facemask when using aerosol or airbrushed paint.

The cost of ready-painted OO-scale figures from Bachmann Scenecraft or Noch generally works out at about £1 per figure. Preiser figures are usually more detailed and are sometimes more expensive. The cost of one unpainted figure from Preiser works out at less than £2 per figure, while unpainted figures from companies such as Dart Castings range from about £1.50 each.

IMPROVING PLASTIC ROAD VEHICLES

There are many companies now producing excellent models of road vehicles in various scales. In OO scale, for example, die-cast road vehicle ranges include those from Bachmann Scenecraft,

Cararama, Classix, EFE, Hornby Skale Autos, Oxford Diecast and a lot more. In addition to these, many European and American manufacturers produce model road vehicles from plastic, either as a ready-made model or as a kit. For example Atlas, Herpa, Rietze and Wiking produce ready-made plastic vehicles, whilst Kibri makes a large number of plastic kits of a variety of road vehicles. The better-quality plastic road vehicles are well detailed and some come with add-on parts such as door mirrors.

Though many plastic model road vehicles are HO scale rather than OO scale, by carefully positioning HO road vehicles on a layout – ideally not next to OO-scale road vehicles – the vehicles do not look out of place. Improving the appearance of a road vehicle does not take too long and it does elevate the look of the model, rather than having it appear to be in ex-showroom condition.

TOOLS AND MATERIALS

Tools required for improving a plastic road vehicle consist of:

- A small paintbrush for painting the parts that benefit from repainting.
- An old small paintbrush for painting Humbrol Maskol on the windscreen and windows.
- A sharp craft knife for cutting the detail parts from the plastic sprues.
- A pair of fine-nosed tweezers for fitting the detail parts.
- A self-sealing cutting board to cut out the number plates.
- Black felt-tipped pen for colouring the edging of the number plates.
- A steel ruler for cutting the number plates.
- A PC and printer for printing the number plates.

Materials required:

- Plastic cement for fixing the mirrors.
- Quick setting adhesive for fixing the number plates.
- Maskol masking fluid.
- Weathering chalks and/or aerosol.

STEP BY STEP CHANGES TO IMPROVE THE APPEARANCE OF A PLASTIC LORRY

Usually lorries, buses and coaches come with detailing parts to be added, such as door mirrors. These need to be cut off the plastic sprue then glued to the model. The job is a little fiddly but a pair of fine-nosed tweezers does help to carry the small mirrors to the holes in the body. Once the parts are pushed in as far as they will go, dribble a small blob of plastic cement around the connection to be certain that the added parts will not fall off.

Before weathering a vehicle, the windows need to be masked. This can be done either by carefully cutting low-tack masking tape and placing it into the windows, or by using Humbrol Maskol fluid, which needs to be carefully 'painted' on to the windows, left to dry and peeled off after the weathering is complete. Weathering a road vehicle can be carried out with weathering chalks, or very light sprays of acrylic paint from an aerosol or airbrush. Go lightly, so as not to make it look too dirty. A micro-paintbrush can be used for painting the indicators and lights on the vehicle.

Three plastic road vehicles in HO scale by Herpa, Rietze and Wiking. There is a huge selection of European road vehicles available, from cars to the largest HGVs. Most of them look a bit too glossy to be realistic straight out of the box, but they can be improved by just one hour's work.

The Wiking MAN lorry used for this demonstration cost £14. The little acrylic paint used cost, say 50p, with a few drops of adhesive at 10p, 15p worth of Maskol and printing ink for the number plates at roughly 10p, bringing the conversion cost to less than £1. From start to finish, including weathering the lorry, adding the mirrors and the number plates, took less than an hour, plus the drying times for the paint and the adhesive. There are various additional projects that could be undertaken to improve this vehicle further, including the addition of a driver.

This concrete lorry is the basis of this project. It looks too clean and shiny.

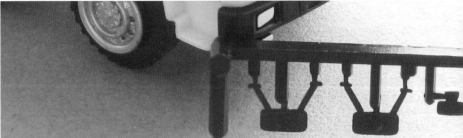

The black plastic sprue containing the three door mirrors. The smaller mirror is fixed on top of the driver's door.

Before weathering the vehicle, the windscreen and side pictures need to be covered with Humbrol Maskol, which can be spread on with an old paintbrush, then left to dry to become rubbery within a few minutes.

After weathering, the Maskol can be carefully peeled off, but be careful not to scratch the plastic windows as you do this. The Maskol comes off quite easily.

The lorry is now showing signs of light weathering after the door mirrors have been fitted. This completed lorry looks much more realistic after just one hour's work.

After the number plate has been added, the model looks so much more complete and realistic. I used UHU quick-setting adhesive to fix the number plate to the vehicle.

There are many companies now producing excellent models of road vehicles in various scales. In OO scale, for example, die-cast road vehicle ranges include those from Bachmann Scenecraft, Classix, Cararama, EFE Hornby Skale Autos, Oxford Diecast and a lot more. This Land Rover is a Hornby Skale Autos model.

This Noch mini-tractor comes complete with its driver in HO scale.

Die-cast cars chase the train on the Wisbech and Upwell Tramway in OO scale. On roads there are a lot of details that can be added, such as road markings, traffic signs (of the correct era), bus stops, car parks, level crossings, road name boards, drain covers, streetlights, pavements, fences, hedges, cyclists, puddles, speed cameras, changes in the road surface, men at work digging up the road, traffic cones, zebra crossings, buses, cars, lorries and the occasional horse-drawn vehicle.

Number Plates

Editable OO-scale number plates are available from Model Railway Scenery (www.modelrailwayscenery.com). These number plates feature subtle weathering, are accurately scaled from the DVLA specifications, have 1200dpi resolution for good results on most printers and are fully compatible with die-cast and plastic kit vehicle models.

TARBET – A SCOTTISH REGION DIORAMA

This small layout only measures 1.3 x 0.4m, but as somewhere to experiment with modelling ideas and as a photographic backdrop it has proved to be very useful.

Class 26 locomotives used to work in Scotland. This one carries the Eastfield depot Scottie dog logo.

Weathered Heljan 26024 locomotive arrives with a closed Railfreight van.

A point level has been added simply by folding and painting a staple.

Before... The lone tree and resin building look distinctly unrealistic.

After... By adding a photographic back scene, a fence, hedging and better ground cover, the scene is transformed.

CHAPTER THIRTEEN

MATERIALS

What is the right material for the job?

In this chapter we will look at the various, and increasing, selection of modelling materials that is available. Some materials have been around in the hobby for a long time, while others are more recent innovations.

WORKING WITH PLASTIC

One of the main building materials used in model-making today is plastic. It is easy to work with and is freely available. Plastic has been a popular choice with kit manufacturers, although laser-cut wood and laser-cut card is becoming increasingly popular and many more building kits are using laser-cut technology rather than solely relying on plastic components.

Styrene (which is short for polystyrene) is generally inexpensive and is available in a number of shapes and sizes in both sheet and strip material. In addition to being used for building structures, it can be used to make rolling stock, buildings and details, as well as having many other uses on a layout.

Plastic card of different thicknesses and textures can be bought from model shops and hobby shops. Strips are available in various dimensions, such as square, rectangular cross sections, rods, tubes, half-rounds, I-beams, Ls and other special shapes such as girders. There are also sheets of brick walling, stone walling, roof tiles, cobbles, road surfaces, pavements and much more. These are available from a number of companies, including Evergreen Scale Models, Plastruct, Slater's, Sylmasta and Wills.

Firms such as DPM, Ratio, Walthers and Wills make a variety of plastic accessories, such as doors,

There are a lot of model huts available as laser-cut card, plastic, laser-cut timber and downloadable paper in the popular scales.

windows, guttering and so on. Wills also makes walling and roofing pieces in a variety of textures.

There are a lot of firms producing plastic-based building kits, including Atlas, Cooper Craft, Dapol (the old Airfix kits), DPM, Faller, Heljan, Kibri, Peco, Pikestuff, Ratio, Walthers and Wills.

WORKING WITH ADHESIVES

Plastic cement or plastic solvent is suitable for building plastic models, including buildings and wagon kits. These adhesives are solvents that dissolve a layer of plastic on each piece and weld the two together. Some prefer to apply the solvent with a brush so that it runs along the join. It is available in tubes, bottles and special dispensers with fine tubes for pinpoint gluing. It sets quickly, but takes up to eight hours to fix finally. Some adhesives set quicker than others. It can leave a slight shiny gloss where excess cement is applied to a joint or any stray cement is left on the kit.

There are various adhesives that are good for working with plastic – these include Deluxe Materials Plastic Magic, Humbrol Liquid Poly, Mek-Pak, Plastic Weld and Revell Contacta. Contact adhesive such as UHU can be used on some plastics, especially where the plastic needs to be fixed to another material, such as cardboard or wood. Cyanoacrylate adhesive (CA) works well for joining plastic to other materials, such as wood, brass and resin. This is also commonly known as 'super glue', with a setting time that is usually between five and sixty seconds and a relatively short curing time of two hours.

There are a great number of plastic building parts available, such as these from Evergreen, Plastruct and Wills.

A self-sealing cutting board, a steel ruler, craft knife plus spare blades and your favourite type of adhesive are the necessary starting points for working with plastic.

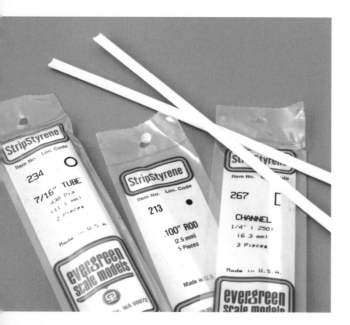

CLOCKWISE FROM TOP LEFT:

Evergreen plastic is available as tubes, rods, channels, H girders and many more types.

It has become almost too easy for modellers to buy ready-to-run wagons these days, but there is still a wide variety of excellent wagon kits available, such as this one by Parkside Dundas.

Plastic kits are readily available for buildings (small and large) and accessories.

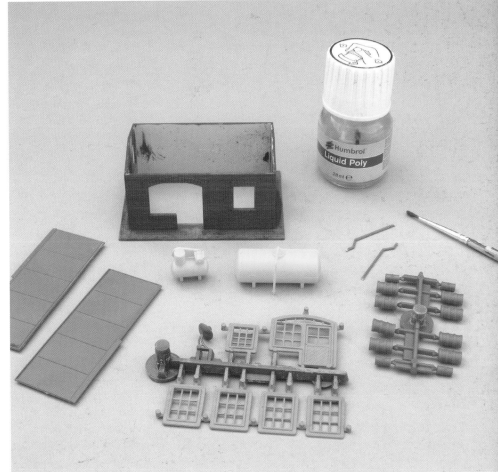

CLOCKWISE FROM TOP LEFT:

Here are some of the DPM modular sections that enable any size and shape of warehouse to be made.

This Shell garage was made from a Piko plastic kit that cost less than £20. Whilst it is based on a European prototype, it could look equally at home on a UK layout.

It is always easier to paint the detail parts (such as the windows) of a plastic kit on the sprue rather than on the assembled model.

Tips for Working with Plastic

- Get familiar with the huge range of plastic products that are available and try working with a small plastic kit before tackling a large structure. This will give you the experience of working with the different techniques (using adhesive and painting) associated with plastic.
- Use a steel ruler and a self-sealing cutting board when cutting any plastic parts. Make an initial cutting stroke to mark the place to be cut, then work with firmer cutting strokes to cut through the plastic. Unless the plastic is very thin, multiple passes of the blade will be necessary. Use only sharp craft knife blades when working with plastic. Blades that are blunt will require more pressure and more cutting strokes. They may also be prone to leaving the cutting line and damaging the rest of the plastic and will not cut cleanly. Blunt blades are also not very safe to work with.
- One of the easiest ways to cut large pieces of styrene is to score a firm line on the plastic with a sharp hobby knife, then bend the sheet at the scoring line so that it snaps, leaving a clean break.

- Use wet & dry paper, a sharp craft knife or a small file to smooth any rough edges after the plastic is cut. Do this cleaning-up work before painting and assembling the parts of a kit.
- If you are scratch-building a structure larger than a hut it is worth supporting the exterior walls with bracing made from triangular pieces of plastic. Kit-built structures do not usually require any additional strengthening.
- Either acrylic or enamel paints can be used to paint plastic. When building a kit it is best to paint most of the parts while still on the plastic sprues. They can always be touched up afterwards if need be on the finished model.
- Wipe off any excess adhesive with a damp cloth before the adhesive sets. If you do not do this, the kit will be left with a shiny patch. Once you are happy with the final appearance of your building or structure, spray the entire model with matt varnish (masking any glazing) – this will protect the paint and hide any glossy spots of excess adhesive.

WORKING WITH CARDBOARD

Cardboard is a modeller's traditional material, but despite the recent innovations it still has many uses. There are various types of cardboard available and some come free, such as cereal packets (apart from the cost of the cereals, that is). New domestic white goods usually arrive in corrugated cardboard. The thicker types of cardboard are ideally suited to making the scenery formers on a layout. Back scenes can be painted on cardboard – mounting card is ideal for this purpose because it bends around corners.

In addition, cardboard of different thicknesses and qualities can be bought from hobby shops and art shops. Mounting card for use in picture framing is a good-quality cardboard that is easily obtained from art shops in a number of sizes and colours. It has a huge number of uses on a model railway layout, including making platforms and roads. When modelling industrial sidings, mounting cardboard can be used to represent

the concrete or tarmac between and alongside the rails. Card can form the basis of pavements when used with paving paper, such as that in the Superquick range.

Laser-cut card is now being used on a lot of building and detailing accessories. It is versatile and can look very realistic. Foamboard is another alternative to cardboard.

CARDBOARD BUILDING KITS

Some firms, such as Superquick, have been producing cardboard-based building kits for over forty years. Other building-kit companies appeared later, such as Metcalfe Models, who are busy introducing lots of new kits at this time. Some of their latest kits include laser-cut parts.

PVA glue is good for sticking card together, but there is now a choice of quicker-setting PVA-based adhesives on the market, including Busch Laser Cut adhesive, Deluxe Materials Roket Card Glue and UHU Holz Leim (retailed by Noch dealers).

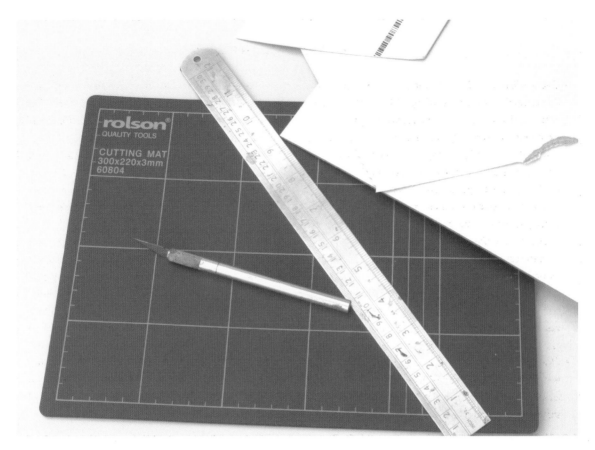

Cardboard comes in many different thicknesses and finishes. Card is still a very valuable part of the modeller's materials. Some cardboard, such as that on cereal packets, comes free, as long as you normally eat breakfast cereals.

Use fine glass paper to smooth any rough edges after the card is cut and before the assembly of the parts.

MAKING STATION PLATFORMS FROM CARDBOARD

Metcalfe retails platform kits for OO and N scales. These versatile kits can be built as straight, curved or island platforms. Pre-cut components enable a box-type structure to give rigid realistic platforms. One kit has enough components to build a platform up to 2.1m (7ft) in length. Other manufacturers that retail cardboard kit-built platforms are Superquick and Scalescenes, using downloaded sheets.

Platforms can be scratch-built using cardboard with brick or stone pattern papers or plastic sheet on the platform walls. To build a platform using cardboard the first step is to decide upon the size of the platform. This is usually a compromise between the length that you would really like and the length that your layout room will permit. If making a curved platform, make a template of the platform using several pieces of white A4 paper stuck together with Sellotape. Press the paper on to the rails so that the rails make an indentation on the paper to give the shape of the platform edge. Cut around these marks to use this as a template to make the shape of the platform. Another way of making a template is to place the paper between the tracks and run your largest carriages around the track by hand, holding a pencil at one corner of the carriage to mark the maximum size of the platform.

Once you are happy that your paper template is the correct size, place it on a piece of mounting card and draw around it with a pencil to transfer the shape of the platform top on to the cardboard. Remember to add extra length each end for the platform ramps. Cut out the desired platform shape using a self-sealing cutting board and a sharp craft knife. By working slowly with a new blade you will be able to follow a curved line. Once the platform shape has been cut out, test it and then use sandpaper to smooth any ragged edges.

Next, make the platform sides. Use a carriage to test the correct height – remember that passengers usually need to step up a little to get into the carriage. Cut out two pieces of mounting card to run along the entire length of the platform, including the ramps. Cut out additional pieces of card that are the same height to the sides to run under the platform along the middle (front to back) of the platform to give it strength and to ensure that it does not sag. Cut the angle of the platform side pieces of card for the ramps. Score the underside of the platform at the top of the ramp and carefully fold down the top to follow the angle of the ramp.

Deluxe Materials Roket Card Glue adhesive or any of the other quick-setting adhesives, such as a contact adhesive, are good for fixing the upright pieces of card to the platform top. Hold them in place with your fingers for a minute or so, until the adhesive starts to set. Leave the glue to dry and ensure that the walls stay at right angles to the platform surface. Then glue in the platform supports and again wait to dry.

Make sure that the cardboard is free from dust, then paint the top surface with grey acrylic paint. Two coats may be needed to cover it fully. For a warning line, use Tamiya low-tack masking tape along the edge to work to. Work your way along the platform face steadily to ensure that the masking tape has a smooth rather than an uneven curve or straight line. Next, paint white acrylic paint to represent the warning line. Two coats are usually necessary if you need a fairly solid white line. Within a few minutes of painting the second coat, remove the tape before the paint dries. Leave it all to dry before positioning it on the layout.

This platform was made from mounting card. The wall is covered with Scalescenes brick paper. The platform surface was painted with grey acrylics and the line painted with white paint, using masking tape for straightness. The buildings are of Shillingstone station by Bachmann Scenecraft.

Mounting card, contact adhesive, masking tape, a cutting board, a steel ruler, a sharp craft knife and stone or brick paper are all that is needed to make a platform, plus the paints and a glue stick to fix the brick paper to the wall.

The underside of a platform showing the strengthening pieces of cardboard on the underside so that it will not sag over time.

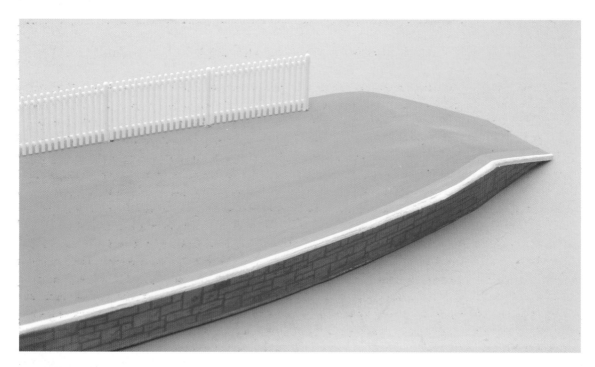

The top of the platform was painted with grey acrylic paint, then the line brown line (representing the edging slabs) was added and later the white line was painted in a two-stage process using masking tape. The fence is by Ratio.

A completed platform made from cardboard with various accessories from the Hornby Skaledale range.

Tips for Working with Card

- Use the correct cardboard for the job. Thin postcards or business cards are ideal for detailing buildings such as window frames, but are not strong enough to form the walls of a building. White goods packing corrugated card might be useful for making scenery formers, but will not be suitable for flat walls on buildings because of their slightly rippled effect. Support the interior walls of a card-built building with bracing made from triangular pieces of cardboard if the building is larger than a hut.
- Try your hand at working with a small structure before tackling a large structure. Always use a steel ruler and a self-sealing cutting board when cutting card. Use only sharp blades when working with card. Blades that are past their best will require more pressure and more cutting strokes. They may also leave ragged edges and are dangerous to work with.
- Have a damp cloth to hand when modelling with card. It can be used for wiping off any excess glue on the finished face of a building – if the glue is not wiped off it will leave a glossy mark that will spoil the look of the finished building.
- Felt-tip pens or a thin wash of acrylic paint can colour and hide any exposed card edges, which are usually at the corners of the buildings or inside the door and window frames. Humbrol washes are another good way to hide the colour of the cut cardboard.
- Brick papers can look good, but need to be applied to card carefully or else they are likely to bubble. Never use neat PVA with brick papers. Use spray mount, diluted PVA or a glue stick. Watch for any air bubbles that occur as the paper is applied and remove them immediately. Using a wallpaper roller is one way to remove any air bubbles.

WORKING WITH REDUTEX SHEETS

Redutex is a Spanish company that has created a patented method of manufacturing textured sheets for modellers. These are available from Model Textures and several other companies in the UK. The sheets have a 3D texture and are pre-coloured in either standard single-colour finish or polychromatic multicoloured finishes. The three standard sheet sizes are scale-dependent. For N and OO scales, the sheets measure 300 x 120mm. All the sheets are generally in landscape format except for the corrugated textures, which are available in both landscape and portrait formats. All sheets come with self-adhesive backing that can be repositioned several times to obtain perfect alignment. After twenty-four hours, the fix becomes semi-permanent.

Because the material is acrylic it can be weathered, dry-brushed or painted using normal modelling techniques. The sheets look good straight out of the packet, but if you paint the edges of the cut material this definitely improves the appearance. I find the

Tips for Using Redutex Sheets

- Redutex sheets are available in most scales from 1/200 right through to 1/12 in a huge range of finishes. The sheets are flexible so that they can be stretched and folded. Applying a little gentle heat with hands or a hairdryer makes the material even more pliable.
- The sheets are self-adhesive with a backing sheet. The adhesive backing sticks to any clean and non-greasy surface. The adhesive allows repositioning during assembly and will reach a semi-permanent fix within twenty-four hours.
- It is very easy to work with these sheets. They are easy to cut with good-quality scissors, craft knives and scalpels

material to be very easy to cut using a sharp craft knife over a self-sealing cutting board. The material can be folded around corners to carry on the alignment of the brickwork. For more information go to www.modeltextures.co.uk and www.redutex.com.

A small required toolkit is a sharp craft knife, self-sealing cutting board, a steel ruler and a pencil for marking up the texture sheet. Also needed is a little matt acrylic paint to 'paint' the edges of the Redutex sheets and Tamiya fine sandpaper to smooth any cut imperfections.

ADHESIVES FOR MODELLERS

There are many things that modellers do that involve using some form of glue (also known as adhesive). These include working with cardboard, plastics, laser-cut card and wood, Redutex sheets, scale timber and multiple materials. Modellers usually have a few types of glue in their toolbox, but which are the best types for a modeller's basic toolkit? What should be considered before buying glue? The main criteria to bear in mind when choosing glues are:

Just some of the huge range of adhesives now available to modellers including hot glue guns, PVA, scenic glues, tacky glues, spray adhesives and hairsprays.

- To select the right glue for the job so that it will give a durable result; for example, if you choose a plastic cement to work with laser-cut wood, the fix will never happen.
- To use a glue that you are comfortable with; some adhesives are more difficult to work with than others and personal choice might be involved.
- To be aware of the safety guidelines for using and storing glues.

It is worth mentioning that it is a good idea to read the directions on the container or packing even before buying the glue. This might prevent you buying the wrong glue. For example, some glue is right for working with cardboard, some is not.

Never use too much glue because it will squeeze out of the joint and cause a bubble of dried adhesive. Use tweezers for putting small pieces in place. Use a fine point to apply a small amount of controlled adhesive. Masking tape can be used to hold together pieces whilst they dry.

Only use the glue as directed in the instructions. If the glue is used in a way not recommended by the manufacturer it might result in a very poor fix, if it works at all. Do not leave glues lying around, especially where there are children or pets in the house.

WHICH IS THE RIGHT ADHESIVE FOR THE JOB?

Ballast glue This is a relatively new arrival on the market and is invaluable when ballasting. It does not need to be mixed with wetting agents and can be used straight from the bottle as an adhesive that runs easily and quickly through ballast.

Contact adhesive This is medium-strength water-resistant glue for general use. It normally takes between five to twenty minutes to set and has a curing time of up to twelve hours. This adhesive dries clear and is suitable for working with cardboard, timber, metal and styrene.

Double-sided tape, sticky fixers and glue dots These are useful where things need to be held in place temporarily.

Glue guns These are available in a range of sizes – some are rather delicate craft glue guns, whilst others are heavy duty for builders. There are two types of glue used: hot glue, which gives the strongest result, but might be more hazardous to use; and cool-melt glue, which operates at a lower temperature and so is less hazardous (but still needs to be used with caution). Replacement glue sticks are readily available. Folks who use glue guns tend to become their greatest advocates.

Plastic cement This is used when building plastic models, including cars, aeroplanes and railway wagon kits. Styrene is the most common plastic in model kits. These adhesives are solvents that dissolve a layer of plastic on each piece and weld the two together. They are available in tubes, bottles and special dispensers with fine tubes for pinpoint gluing. They set quickly, but take up to eight hours to fix finally.

PVA glue This is probably the most versatile and commonly used glue in the model railway layout building and scenery-making process. It is widely available in DIY stores, craft shops, stationers, supermarkets and discount shops. It is generally known as 'white glue'. It comes in various strengths, ranging from light-tack craft PVA, to wood glue, through to exterior-building quality. The price range of the glue is enormous – it is sold in small plastic bottles (that work out to be very expensive), right through to 5ltr buckets. Frequently at DIY stores it is seen in 1ltr and 0.5ltr plastic bottles. PVA glue can be used for timber, wood products, cardboard, paper, plaster and some fabrics. As its common name of White Glue suggests, it is a white liquid, but generally dries clear. The exterior-building quality PVA is sometimes yellow and does dry yellow, so must be used with caution in the hobby. Wood glue and exterior-grade PVA are stronger than standard or craft PVA, so both are recommended for baseboard construction. PVA starts to sets in fifteen to sixty minutes, but needs twenty-four hours to reach its maximum strength.

Scenic glues These are usually PVA-based and are useful both for the fixing of scatters and foliage, but also as a sealer to the scenery once all the layers of scatter materials have been applied. Applying a layer prevents loose scatter materials falling off a baseboard during transit.

Spray glues These come in repositionable and permanent types. They are often known as mounting glue and are sold in aerosols. The permanent type is usually best for layouts. These dry transparent and can be used to fix scatter materials to the landscape, foam foliage to trees and as a final sealing bond for the ground cover. Cheap unscented extra-hold hairspray works relatively well for these tasks too and is available at less than 90p per aerosol.

Super glue This instant-setting glue is for repairing china and much more. Cyanoacrylate adhesives are excellent for joining metal to metal and metal to almost anything else. The setting time is usually between five and sixty seconds, with a relatively short curing time of two hours.

Three of the large number of adhesives for working with plastics. Sometimes the adhesive you choose will be the one you have had the most success with before.

Specialized glues for working with laser-cut card are available. These two are fast-setting and I find them to be versatile for many modelling tasks, such as fixing figures to the layout.

Spray adhesives are especially useful when working with foliage, hedges and trees. The prices vary from around 75p for extra-hold unscented hairspray to £10 for professional spray adhesive.

When ballasting track, PVA is frequently used. It needs some drops of washing-up liquid or Super Wet to assist it to run through dry ballast quickly and evenly.

This is just a selection of the adhesives available in 2015 for planting static grass fibres on a layout.

Acrylic paints are readily available from hobby and art shops. Woodland Scenics retails a range of landscape earth colours too.

Safety Tips When Using Adhesives

- Many adhesives and their fumes can irritate eyes, skin and nose. Read the instructions carefully for safe use of the product.
- Work in a well-ventilated area and replace the cap on the bottles as soon as possible to reduce the escape of fumes.
- Be especially careful when using super glues. They can fix your fingers or other body parts together. Get medical attention immediately if something goes wrong.

MODERN MATERIALS

In the last couple of years static grass fibres suitable for N scale have become available. Depicted here are 1mm static grass fibres that are suitable for Z- and N-scale layouts.

Gravestones in 4mm are available as laser-cut parts from True Texture.

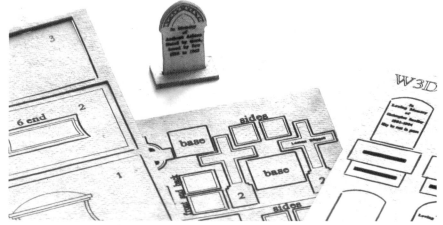

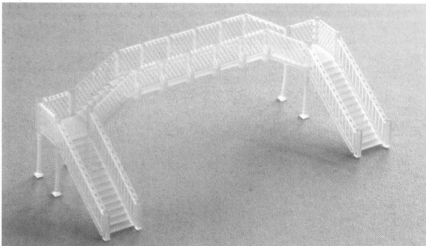

This N-scale footbridge, based on Kirby, is supplied in a 3D frosted finish that requires painting after washing the model in warm soapy water. The matt translucent plastic material features fine detail. The level of detail is superb. To see more, go to www.shapeways. com/shops/ modelrail.

Albion Alloys metal parts are very useful for kit-bashers and scratch-builders.

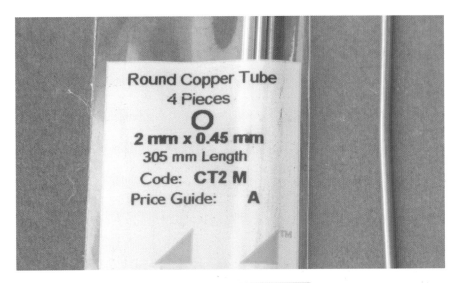

Grass mats have never been so good. Long gone are those bright green ones with very short fibres.

Never have there been so many glues available for modellers.

CHAPTER FOURTEEN

BUILDINGS

A little work makes your buildings look very different.

A couple of decades ago, the choice of buildings for modellers was limited. There were cardboard kits and plastic kits and the only alternative was to build your own. Now we also have a range of downloadable kits, laser-cut kits and ready-made resin buildings. In addition, there are a lot of laser-cut parts available for the scratch-builder.

IMPROVING RESIN BUILDINGS

For some years now it has been possible to buy many types of buildings and accessories made from resin in well-detailed fully assembled form in both OO and N scales. These are real time savers if you are prepared to have a building on your layout that will look similar to the building on a layout of another

modeller. Ready-assembled buildings made from polyresin are a very good way to make a low-relief town, a farm, small town, coal mine or station quickly. These buildings do not require painting or assembly and are available from a number of companies, including Bachmann Scenecraft in both OO and N scale, Harburn Hobbies (Harburn Hamlet), Hornby (Skaledale for OO scale) and Scenix.

The Bachmann Scenecraft range is one of the largest and includes, for example, locomotive depots, a coal mine, an art deco station, footbridges, goods sheds, signal boxes, warehouses, houses, office blocks, bus depot, a container terminal crane, a milk depot, low-relief buildings and many more. In addition, models are made of preserved stations such as Highley and Shillingstone.

This warehouse was 'kit-bashed' using DPM and Pikestuff kits. The DPM modular pieces were used for the brown part of the building. The Pikestuff kit was for a modern diesel locomotive shed that was cut in half and used as a loading bay.

Another building made from a Pikestuff kit that has been adapted from a locomotive shed and painted, then weathered. Additional pipes and so on are plastic tubing.

The warehouse is by US company Atlas and the loading shed is by Pikestuff. Both have been 'Anglicized'.

PERSONALIZING YOUR BUILDINGS

The buildings can be used straight out of the box, but it is always best to personalize them, which can include adding signs or posters to industrial, office or station buildings as a quick way to make the building 'bespoke' to your layout. Various companies sell miniature signs and posters in all the popular scales. These include Gaugemaster, Sankey Scenics and Trackside Signs. Alternatively, why not make your own bespoke signs using a digital camera and scaling them up or down on your PC and printing them at home?

Weathering with acrylic paints or weathering chalks makes a huge difference to the appearance of a building. After all, what building in real life is not weathered by age? Adding interior lights using the Hornby Skale Lighting system or doll's house lights means that your layout gains life if you run it with the room lights dimmed. It is necessary to black out the interior walls of the buildings because light does shine through resin.

Attach weeds and creeping ivy to the walls by using one of the foliage mats available from Busch, Heki, miniNatur, Noch and Woodland Scenics. The material is easy to tear off from the main piece and tease out to suit the area that you need to cover – use a few drops of PVA glue to fix it to the wall. As the adhesive is drying, use your fingers to sprinkle on fine scatter material to soak up any excess adhesive. Climbing roses and other flowering rambling plants can be made easily by teasing out some of the coloured texture foliage mats sold by the 4D Modelshop and other companies. Laser-cut rambling roses made from thin laser-cut card are now available from Noch. A couple of pots with plants either side of the front door of a cottage make a nice little touch. Such pots are available ready planted from Gaugemaster and Noch. Just put a dab of PVA adhesive on to the base of the pot and position it in place.

If you are using a row of the same type of cottage or house, just painting the doors different colours using a small paintbrush with acrylic paints will make a huge visual difference. You may need a couple of coats of paint to cover the original. Use a fine or micro-paintbrush. Adding curtains to some of the windows is a good way to make your buildings different to those seen on other layouts. Curtains or blinds can be made from scraps of different-coloured paper, thin card or tissue. Contact

Bachmann is working with various heritage lines to produce a selection of Scenecraft buildings for both N and OO scales. These include buildings from the Bluebell Railway, the Great Central Railway, the North Dorset Railway Trust and Severn Valley Railway. This model is based on Shillingstone station as it appeared in June 2013. CHRIS NEVARD/MODEL RAIL

The Skaledale cottage on the left is untouched. The one to the right has had curtains added and looks much more realistic.

This concrete works by Bachmann Scenecraft has been weathered with dyes and real sand was sprinkled on to a little matt varnish.

Bedding in resin ready-painted buildings is very important. Static grass fibres and real sand was sprinkled on to spread PVA adhesive to mask the tiny gap between the building and the land.

Resin ready-made buildings provide a quick way of adding an industry to a layout in OO and N scale. Here is the Bachmann Scenecraft Brewery.

The Shillingstone signal box and plate-layer hut are straight out of the box by Bachmann Scenecraft.

adhesive or Sellotape can be used to fix the curtains in place inside the building and having some curtains open and some closed adds visual variety. Net curtains can be made from light tissue paper. Windows can be made to look dirty by scrubbing them with sandpaper or dribbling diluted watercolours down them. If you brush liquid poly on to the windows they will turn frosty for a wintry scene. Cutting the windows is quite easy to do with a sharp craft knife so as to create the illusion of a broken pane, which looks good on industrial buildings in a rundown area.

Resin cuts quite cleanly with a sharp saw, which makes the possibility of 'kit-bashing' buildings simple by adding extensions using plastic card or laser-cut timber. Alternatively, sometimes two resin buildings can be joined together. To extend a resin building it is worthwhile using texture material such as that by Redutex. It does not matter too much that it will not be exactly the same colour as that of the main building, because extensions rarely feature the identical-colour brick or stonework.

Some of the US manufacturers, including Woodland Scenics, produce ready-built plastic buildings. These are known as 'built-ups'. These buildings are usually made from plastic and, once weathered, they look quite good, so long as you chose a building that does not look out of place on a UK layout.

WEATHERING RESIN BUILDINGS

Within a few years of a real building being erected it starts to look a little dirty or tired. Resin buildings straight out of the box look good, but can look even better by using a few simple techniques. Start by studying photographs of real buildings to see what effects you need to reproduce. Weathering the roofs is one of the most important things to do because these catch the eye first. This can be done by dry-brushing. To do this, use a flat paintbrush just dipped into acrylic paint. Take off any excess paint with a kitchen tissue. Brush up and down gently along the roof tiles. Some paint will stick to the raised detail on the tiles. Once the paint has been applied, partially rub it off using a tissue so that the weathering remains between the tiles. Roofs, particularly in coastal areas, might see various amounts of bird droppings from

the ridge which can be reproduced with a little white paint on the tip of a paintbrush.

The walls of a building can be weathered using dry-brushing, or this can also be done using an airbrush, charcoal or chalk pastels. Running some diluted watercolour paints through the brick or stone courses will immediately create highlights. Using weathering dyes is another method. These dyes are water- or alcohol-soluble and provide good adhesion even on glossy paint finishes and smooth metals. They dry matt and can be sprayed with an airbrush, or brushed on with a flat paintbrush. Starting at the top of buildings, use thin washes of the dyes and, as with the other methods, let the diluted dye drip down through the brickwork. Humbrol's washes are yet another good way to weather buildings. The Humbrol website has a good video demonstrating how to do this.

With all weathering techniques, unless you want your building to look very dirty go easy on them. You can always add additional weathering later, but it is not so easy to take layers of dirt off.

WORKING WITH DOWNLOADABLE KITS

During the last few years, several companies have introduced kits that can be purchased on the Internet, then downloaded and printed at home using your PC and printer. The printed paper then needs to be stuck to cardboard during the assembly process.

Model Railway Scenery, Scalescenes and Smart Models are just three of these Internet-based enterprises that have expanded the growing range of building-card kits, enabling the creation of structures that can easily be modified to suit individual modeller's requirements. The kits offer good value for money, though of course the cost of your own printing ink does need to be added to the price of the kit, in addition to the cardboard.

These companies also produce an increasing range of ships, boats, road surfaces, brick and stone papers and much more, so are useful for the scratch-builder or kit-basher. If you want to try one of their kits before buying, there are various sample kits available on their websites that are free of charge. These are three of the companies that retail such kits:

- www.modelrailwayscenery.co.uk.
- www.scalescenes.com.
- www.smartmodels.co.uk.

TOOLS AND MATERIALS

Tools and materials needed for making downloadable kits consist of:

- An aerosol of matt varnish to seal the model at the finish.
- Diluted acrylic paints for painting the exposed edges of the paper and cardboard.
- A black felt-tipped pen for colouring the exposed edges of the cut paper and cardboard.
- A colour printer with a supply of spare ink cartridges.
- A good-quality glue stick (one that has not dried out).
- An Internet connection and a PC.
- PVA adhesive where the glue stick is not suitable.
- Scatter material, real sand or static grass fibres to hide the join between the building and the baseboard.
- A self-sealing cutting board.
- Small paintbrushes for painting the exposed edges of the paper and cardboard.
- A steel ruler for cutting the paper and cardboard.
- A supply of good-quality paper.

HOW TO USE DOWNLOADABLE KITS

The stage by stage process starts by visiting the website and choosing the item(s) that you want to purchase. Make your payment online and the PDF file(s) may then be downloaded via an email that will be sent to you. Usually two PDF files are received to download. One of these is the kit comprising of several A4 full colour pages. The other PDF contains illustrated A4 instructions. The instructions are easy to follow and there is a common set of symbols that are used. Once the files are downloaded they can be saved to your computer and printed as many times as you like. The building kits can be ordered

in a variety of photo-based textures, including brick (various colours and bonds), concrete or stone. This is useful because it reduces the chance of your building looking like that of another modeller.

Scalescenes Builder's Yard downloads cover roads, pavements, brickwork, stonework, concrete, arches, furniture and much more. These do not come as two PDFs because the general instructions on how to use these can be found on the Scalescenes website.

In my experience, before you print any of the sheets it will be worthwhile cleaning the print nozzles on your printer to ensure that you get the best possible print quality for the sheets. A poor print quality may ruin your model. It is also best to turn the printer to its 'best quality' print capability to get the best colour reproduction that your printer will produce. Make sure that you have a supply of spare ink cartridges because there is nothing more frustrating than having printed the first sheet to run out of ink and further ink supplies can be days away. Using better-quality paper (photographic paper for signs and so on) rather than economy paper will give a better end result. If the paper has a slight gloss to it, the model can be sprayed with matt varnish on completion.

The printed paper needs to be stuck to cardboard during the assembly process. The detailed instructions will tell you which thickness of card is suitable. Good-quality cardboard is available from art shops or Hobbycraft, though for some parts cereal packets are perfectly adequate. In addition to the kit, you will need a self-sealing cutting board, a sharp craft knife, spare new blades, a glue stick, a steel ruler and a selection of thicknesses of cards. A little acrylic paint will be needed at the end of the assembly process, together with a thick felt-tipped pen (usually black). A matt varnish aerosol is useful also for the last stage in the building process. Read the instructions and work your way through the assembly process step by step before cutting any of the parts.

The instructions will suggest using a glue stick to fix the printed paper on to the backing card. I find that a glue stick works very well indeed, provided that the entire area to be fixed is covered with glue. A glue stick is also useful because it allows a little 'slide' before the glue sets. Ensure that your glue stick is relatively new and has not dried out before you start work on the kit. Replace the blade in your craft knife as soon as it gives any indication of becoming 'tired' because blunt blades can make a mess of cutting the paper.

Bare edges on the cardboard or paper can be coloured using a thick felt-tipped pen or diluted acrylic paints. Drainpipes, guttering and final details can be added from plastic parts and fixed to the building with PVA or contact adhesive.

The PDF files can be printed on your own printer after being downloaded from www.scalescenes.com or one of the other websites that offers downloadable kits.

The kits can usually be ordered in a choice of finishes to make your building as individual as possible.

Scalescenes provides a scale ruler that can be downloaded, which is a useful modelling tool to gauge the height of figures and so on. One of the PDFs to be printed is the instructions for the kit; these are quite easy to follow. All the kits of a particular company will share a common set of symbols.

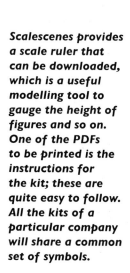

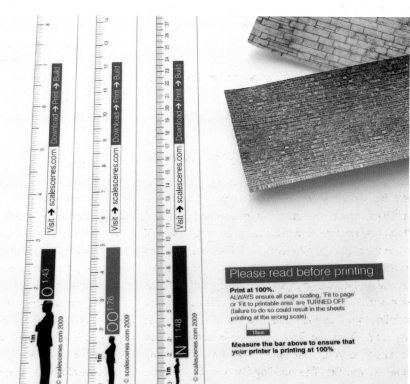

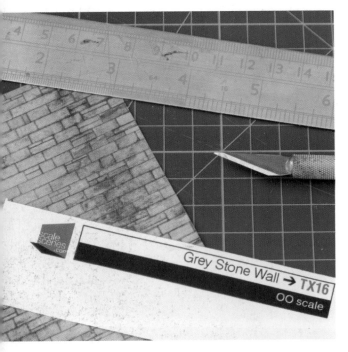

Working with cardboard requires a self-sealing cutting board, a steel ruler and a sharp craft knife (ideally with some spare blades).

In addition to the kit, you will need a cutting board, a sharp craft knife, a glue stick, a steel ruler and a selection of thicknesses of cards.

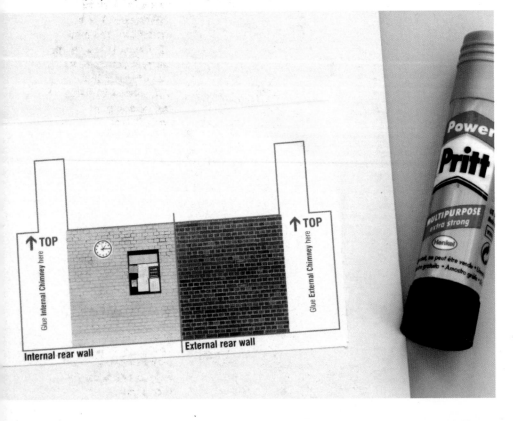

Here, one of the interior walls of a hut has been stuck on to 2mm card using a glue stick.

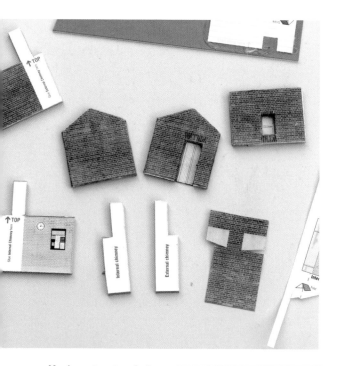

Various parts of the hut before assembly of the walls and roof.

The roof is made up of separate strips of tiling laid on to cardboard, then the ridge tiles are attached. One end of the roof has been cut and finished in this picture. The other end (nearest the camera) is unfinished.

The walls are assembled and the roof is ready to fix into place.

The assembled hut in almost finished state. Drainpipes and guttering are still to be added, along with some touching up of the brickwork.

The fully finished hut. This is the result of two hours' work. The drainpipes are plastic parts left over from other kits. They also hide the join in the brickwork sheets.

This halt building was made from another Scalescenes sheet. These kits obviously take longer to make than a resin ready-painted building, but you have the satisfaction that you built it.

MAKING A LASER-CUT CARD KIT

The Noch range of small building kits includes garden sheds and kiosks. Busch and other companies are also increasingly producing building kits using laser-cut card. Laser-cut card is one of the newer materials now available for modellers and is being used on an increasing number of models. Not only is the card used for buildings and fencing, but also on models of bridges as well as plants and vegetables. Laser-cut card can be delicate, but is also strong.

Noch has a large range of laser-cut bridges. Here are the laid-out parts from one of its simpler bridge kits.

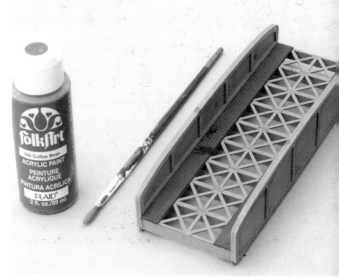

During assembly of the bridge kit acrylic paint was used on the walkway of the bridge.

The laser-cut assembled bridge in situ before the scenery was made up around the location.

ABOVE: *Superbly moulded laser-cut doors and windows from True Texture (www.truetexture.co.uk).*

LEFT: *The finished bridge took just a couple of hours to make. Once you have learned how to assemble laser-cut kits, the next one will be even easier.*

Lots of the big scenery players in Europe make an increasing number of kits using laser-cut technology. This selection of parts is by Faller.

One of the more elaborate bridge kits by Noch. These kits made from laser-cut cardboard are surprisingly robust.

Laser-cut flowers and plants are available from a number of companies and are a good way to add plants to a layout. They do benefit from a light wash of acrylic paint to hide the cut edge of thin cut cardboard.

TOOLS

The tools needed for making laser-cut kits consist of:

• Deluxe Materials Roket Card Glue or UHU Holz Leim Express (these adhesives set faster than PVA adhesive).
• Felt-tipped pens for touching up the edges of the card as necessary.
• Light brown acrylic paints for door frames and window frames.
• A self-sealing cutting board.
• A sharp craft knife with spare blades.
• Small paintbrushes.
• A steel ruler for use when cutting out the glazing or curtains.

MAKING A NOCH LASER-CUT KIT

Some of the latest laser-cut kits from Busch, Noch and other companies add a further novel method of assembly by featuring mitred-cut card for the main walls. Noch's range of laser-cut products is expanding each year. The company is promoting its OO/HO

building kits as different to most other kits on the market because of their ease of assembly. The logo on the box is: 'Glue, Fold – Finished'. But is it really as simple as that?

These kits feature age-resistant cardboard with 45-degree mitred corners on the walls. The corners of the walls need to be glued with the supplied UHU adhesive, then pushed together and held for a few seconds whilst the adhesive dries. The mitred joints ensure that the corner join is not visible, which is a step forwards from traditional card kits. The walls carry a matt finish, while the insides of the walls are finished in black so that if the purchaser decides to add lights he does not need to paint the inside of the building, which is a useful time-saver.

Plastic gutters and drainpipes are included and the roof tiles have been laser-cut. Curtains and glazing are also supplied. The instructions are clear, with text in English and exploded diagrams. The initial range of these buildings by Noch included a station building, a goods shed, a farm scene, a church and a residential house. Some of these buildings are more suitable

The box of the house kit by Noch displaying the 'Glue, Fold – Finished' strapline, which is rather optimistic. These kits are available from www.gaugemaster.com and other Noch dealers.

for UK-based layouts than others. If you omitted to attach the window shutters on this kit house it would not look too much out of place in a UK town setting. The footprint of this building is 120 x 90mm (4¾ x 3½in).

To me, the 'Glue, Fold – Finished' strapline on the box seems a little misleading. That would be correct if you were not intending to fit doors, windows and other details. This kit took me over three hours

to build and most of that time was spent on the window frames, doors, curtains, guttering and weathering. It is true that the basic shell could be assembled within fifteen minutes, but the resultant building would look very austere and plain. Only by adding the details does it begin to look realistic. The mitred corner joints work very well and fitment of the parts throughout is very good indeed. All of the parts are of good quality.

The contents of the kit include parts in laser-cut card and plastic, plus adhesive.

The curtains, window frames and the window surrounds all need to be cut out from the backing sheets using a sharp craft knife over a cutting board.

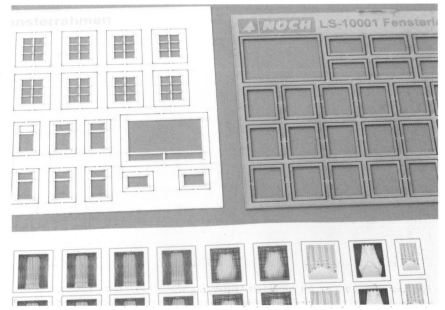

To clean up the edge of the ready-made window apertures use a small craft file. If you do not take off the excess cardboard the window frame will protrude from the wall.

I gave a thin wash of colour to the window surrounds using Tamiya acrylic paint.

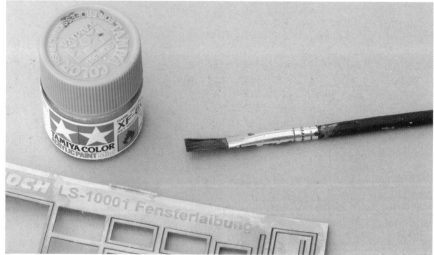

Cutting the window surrounds from the backing card using a sharp craft blade.

CLOCKWISE FROM TOP LEFT:

The paper curtains were cut out from the supplied sheet using a small pair of scissors.

On the inside of each wall the window frames and then the glazing were fixed with small dabs of UHU adhesive. The curtains were added with another dot of adhesive top and bottom. You will need to position the curtains from the viewing side of the model to ensure that they are positioned correctly.

When you are ready to fix the walls in place, give yourself a dry run by holding the walls together before you start applying adhesive.

The chimney comes in a five-part section, which needs to be cut from the backing sheet.

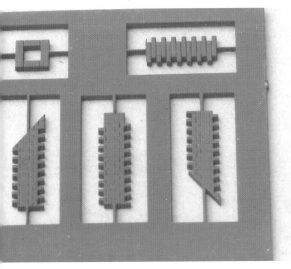

Here is the chimney fixed to the roof. It needs a little patching up of the colour, but this will form part of the weathering process of the entire roof.

The house, complete with drainpipes, flowering window boxes and shutters. The latter two items would not need to be added if the house was used on a UK layout.

The finished house with a fully weathered roof ready for a European-style layout. The building took around three hours to build and detail. The tiles have been rubbed with Tamiya weathering chalks and look so much better than the original bright red roof tiles.

WHAT SKILLS ARE REQUIRED TO BUILD A LASER-CUT KIT?

It is necessary to cut out window frames and other details from their backing sheets. This is easy provided that you have the necessary tools. The window frames and edges of the cardboard will need to be painted with a small paintbrush or felt-tipped pen.

As with the other materials, use a steel ruler and a cutting board when cutting laser-cut card. Use only new blades when working with laser-cut card. Blades that are tired will leave torn edges and will require more cutting strokes. Whilst PVA glue can be used

for sticking laser-cut card together, other adhesives do the job better because they dry quicker. These include: Deluxe Materials Roket Card Glue and UHU Holz Leim Express (available from Noch dealers in the UK). Have a damp cloth alongside you and wipe any excess glue off the model as soon as possible. Set adhesive can sometimes leave a shiny patch on the model.

These are easy kits to build, but your patience might be tested as you cut all those parts from the backing sheets and assemble the windows and glazing in multiple layers.

PLANTING BUILDINGS ON A LAYOUT

The visual impact of a nicely finished building is spoilt if there is a gap running along the lower edge of the building. Models of buildings do need to be carefully fixed to the baseboard to make them look realistic.

PVA or contact adhesive can be used to fix the buildings to the layout and as the glue is drying around the base of the building it is easy to sprinkle on a very fine scatter material that will stick to the drying PVA and hide the join. Alternatively, static grass fibres can be applied to the wet glue with a puffer bottle or an electrostatic grass tool. Static grass has the advantage that the fibres are taller than fine scatter material and will mask any fine gap around the building.

Pavements are another way to improve the realism of model buildings. Metcalfe Models manufactures good self-adhesive paving kits for both OO and N scales. The Metcalfe paving slabs are laid slab by slab. That does sound to be a laborious task, but it is more fun than drudgery. Though the slabs are self-adhesive, it is still worth brushing a little PVA on the underside of the slabs just before fixing them down. The Superquick range includes paving papers in a choice of colours. These can be fixed on to cardboard. Some of the downloadable kit companies such as Scalescenes offer pavement sheets that are easy to work with.

Demolition scenes are the ideal location for models of buildings that you may have built over the years, but which no longer meet your best modelling standards. This scene was at the Nuremberg Toy Fair on the Lädegutter Bauer stand.

SCRATCH-BUILDING A DEPOT BUILDING

Scratch-building is easier than you think and can be very satisfying. Here are the main parts of a Wisbech and Upwell Tramway depot building. The walls are cardboard covered in Scalescenes brick paper. The windows are plastic pieces left over from another kit. The door is laser-cut timber.

Before the roof was added it was possible to see the strengthening pieces of cardboard along the sides of the building.

The finished building after the window sills had been added (balsa wood), the drainpipes (plastic) and the roof (cardboard covered with Scalescenes roofing tiles and ridge tiles).

PENDON'S MAGNIFICENT BUILDINGS

The Pendon Vale scene is inspirational to those who want to model buildings with superb realism.

This farmyard scene at Pendon has all the hallmarks of master modelling at its best.

The Pendon Parva signal box and its surrounding details are what most scratch-builders endeavour to achieve.

With some flowers made from human hair, Pendon's modelling is exquisite.

CHAPTER FIFTEEN

PHOTOGRAPHING YOUR MODELS

Photography is a great aid to better modelling.

The digital age of photography has encouraged more people to record their layouts. Digital cameras give us the chance to click away until we get pictures that we are happy with. The purpose of this section is to assist modellers to get the most out of their photography and maybe to get their layout into print in one of the model railway magazines.

WHY TAKE PICTURES?

I use photographs as an aid to better modelling. For example, studying photos of your models might bring you to the conclusion that you have not included sufficient detail on the layout. You can then work up this detail and take another picture to see if you are pleased with the outcome. You may see a fault in a building and this can then be corrected.

Most magazines have at least one or two pages of 'readers' layouts', consisting of pictures submitted by the builders of their layouts. This is a great

This small layout used 3ltr of PVA adhesive, proving that it always good to have in stock plenty of white glue. CHRIS NEVARD/MODEL RAIL

way to share the layout that you are proud of with other modellers. And, who knows, the magazine might be so taken with your layout that it sends one of its professional photographers to take pictures so that it can be enjoyed by many more to its full glory.

THE ADVANTAGES OF DIGITAL PHOTOGRAPHY

One of the advantages of digital photography is that once you have bought the camera, there is very little future financial outlay. This is so different to the days of paying for film processing. Now you only need to pay printing costs for those pictures that you want to keep as hard-copy photographs. Pictures that you have taken can be stored on your PC or laptop, on a CD, on a tablet, or any other recording device. You can take a whole range of slightly different shots of the same scene to choose the best one for submission to a magazine. The rest of the pictures can be deleted if you want.

Sharing digital images is easy: they can be sent via emails; posted on websites online; printed out on paper; or sent by post on CDs. Most digital cameras have a 'close-up' or 'macro' facility, so that you can take good, crisp pictures of detailed areas of a layout. Compact digital cameras enable all of us to take jolly good photographs, with the camera being small enough to slip into one's trouser pocket.

The cost of digital cameras seems still to be falling, relatively speaking. You still get more equipment the more you pay for a camera, but compared with four to five years ago, even entry-level cameras are now packed with good features.

TAKING PICTURES WITH DIGITAL CAMERAS

Get familiar with your camera and its controls by studying the instruction manual in hard copy or online. Most camera manufacturers have adopted common symbols, so once you have mastered one camera moving on to the next one is not such a challenge.

Whilst it has always generally been better to take pictures of layouts in good daylight, digital cameras are also very good in low light situations. If the layout is permanently located indoors, you might need to use a mixture of daylight and artificial light when taking photographs. There are ways to compensate for artificial lighting on digital cameras – look at your camera's manual to see if you can adjust the White Balance on your camera, which might give you a setting to use to compensate for tungsten, fluorescent or other lighting conditions. Bright sunlight can create shadows that do always give the best results. But if your layout is portable you can learn to work with shadows and shade by slightly turning around a layout or a diorama in the sun until the shadows are hidden.

For model railway photography ideally the camera will have: adjustable shooting modes including Auto, Aperture Priority and Manual; adjustable white light balance, an auto focus facility; a self-timer; and a tripod mounting screw.

A timber-loading siding is a good way to provide railway interest in a corner of a layout. CHRIS NEVARD/MODEL RAIL

A photograph of a diorama taken outside, with the garden used as the background. The busy background of the garden distracts from the modelled scene. A back scene is necessary to focus attention on the modelled scene.

The same diorama with a plain sheet of mounting cardboard as a back scene. This starts to concentrate the eye on the locomotive and the modelled area.

Finally, a photo back scene has been used to complete the scene. Compare the previous two photographs to see what a difference the back scene makes.

Nothing mars a good digital image more than a layer of dust on the layout, which can then be seen in the picture. Use an air puffer to blow away any dust, cat hairs, leftover scatter material or static grass fibres on the layout and rolling stock before taking the pictures. These useful tools can be bought for around £5 from specialist tool suppliers at model railway shows.

It is not necessary to have a back scene fixed on a diorama or layout to photograph it, but it is always best to hide the background. Just a sheet of light blue mounting card will be adequate for this purpose. Large sheets can be purchased from Hobbycraft or any art shops from around £5. I have a personal dislike of seeing the baseboard edge in any picture. Whilst it is unavoidable from time to time, when building a baseboard you may choose to make one that is wider rather than narrower. In this way, there is less chance of the baseboard edge becoming obvious in pictures.

Use the 'macro' or 'close-up' setting on the camera where detail shots are called for. This is usually shown as a tulip on the camera's setting dial. Investing in a tripod is essential to achieve the best-quality photos. Though the best cameras now feature some form of image-stabilization system, this can never be as good as the rock-solid results that a tripod can give.

If your layout is portable and your home has a conservatory with lots of light, this can be useful when the weather outside is unsuitable for photography. Vary the angle from which you take the pictures. Try shooting from below the railway line looking up, across the tracks, from the top of a building and a helicopter shot.

Remember to keep the camera battery topped up. There is nothing more frustrating than setting up a good picture only to see the sunlight fading and the camera closing down because of a flat battery.

It is best to set the camera to take pictures in Superfine quality if you want to see them in print. Whilst this will limit the number of pictures that can be kept on a storage card, the resultant crispness of the picture image will be worth it. Remember to back up your favourite pictures on a CD or another storage device.

TAKING IT TO THE NEXT STAGE

Digital SLR cameras enable the user to take even better pictures, but they do work out to be more expensive and bulky than a compact camera. An in-between option is one of the top of the range compact cameras, such as a Canon G16, which includes such useful features as aperture priority to give the user a lot of control over depth of field (the amount of the photo that remains in focus) and other aspects.

If you wish to see your layout or models in print, send a couple of low-resolution pictures to the editor first to see if he thinks that they will be suitable for publication. He may ask you to send in high-resolution pictures on a CD later.

If your main interest is building and photographing locomotives and rolling stock and your layout is permanently indoors, or you have no layout, why not build a small diorama solely for the purpose of photographing your handiwork. It will be easy to store and to move around.

For more information on photography for modellers, Chris Nevard's excellent four-page article on the subject in the July 2008 issue of *Model Rail* has been in part reproduced on his website. To view the article and some of his superb model photography, may I suggest you visit www.nevard.com.

WHERE CAN I LOOK TO IMPROVE MY SKILLS FURTHER?

VISIT

PENDON MUSEUM

At Pendon Museum the model makers aim to recapture scenes showing the beauty of the English countryside as it used to be around 1930. This is scenic modelling at its very best. A visit to the Museum is inspirational for modellers of all skill levels. The Museum's superbly modelled cottages, gardens, farms, fields and lanes recall the peaceful country ways of that period. This is an ideal family day out.

Pendon Museum
Long Wittenham
Abingdon
Oxon
OX14 4QD

For details of the opening hours and the days the Museum is open go to the website: www.pendonmuseum.com.

A visit to the superb Pendon Museum is a good family day out. It is not only modellers who enjoy the exhibition layouts; other family members will too.

BOOKS

Detailing and Modifying Ready-to-Run Locomotives in OO Scale (Volume 1: British Diesel and Electric Locomotives 1955–2008) is a 92-page book by George Dent covering Tools of the Trade, First Steps in Customizing, Painting, Weathering and lots more. The techniques are well described and depicted. Weathering is discussed from light to downright filthy. All the chapters are well illustrated. The book has a list of useful addresses and a bibliography. Available from Crowood: www.crowood.com.

Peco's *Setrack OO/HO and N Planbooks* are useful small books with plans from tiny layouts to larger ones. The colour illustrations of the plans are excellent. These practical little books begin with a good summary of most of the basic constructional techniques that will be needed by the beginner, including baseboard construction, tracklaying, electrics, control, scenery and suggestions for homes for a model railway. They are available from Peco or any of their retailers. Good value for money and they are updated frequently.

Model Railway Planning and Design Handbook by Paul A. Lunn, Neil Ripley, Ken Gibbons, Jack Burnard and Steve Flint features track plans and 3D drawings of finished projects. Some of the layouts are in the beginner's category, but others are more advanced. A first-class introduction to planning a new layout. This 96-page soft-back book is available from Book Law Publications: www.booklaw.co.uk.

Railway Modelling: The Realistic Way is a 352-page volume by Iain Rice that contains a huge amount of information. Useful for beginners wanting to improve their skills and knowledge through to advanced modellers. A good read for those folk wanting to move towards finescale modelling: www.haynes.co.uk.

Peco's *Shows You How* booklets are useful small guides on specific topics. Cheap to buy and easy to read, they supply quick ways to learn about specific areas of skills for the hobby. They are updated from time to time and cover a wide range of topics, including starting out in OO Gauge, baseboard construction, tracklaying, DCC, scenery and more.

Building a Model Railroad Step by Step is a 112-page book from US publisher Kalmbach that has 250 colour photos and 20 illustrations. The author builds an N-scale layout from scratch. There are a lot of step-by-step photos and illustrations and whilst the layout depicted is a US one, the techniques and principles are good for UK layouts too. In the UK, Model Junction (www.modeljunction.info) and Steam Powered Video (www.spv.co.uk) can supply the book.

Phil's Model Railway Fillets by Phil Parker is a handy sixty-page compilation of miscellaneous articles on a range of model railway topics. The topics covered include building wagons, exhibiting layouts, scratchbuilding and numerous handy tips. Available from www.philsworkbench.co.uk.

Wild Swan modelling books are slim publications of good quality that nicely describe various modelling techniques. The books include *Modelling the GWR*, *Designing a Layout, Landscape Modelling, Making Model Buildings* and so on.

Modelling Grassland and Landscape Detailing; Modelling Deciduous Trees; and *Modelling Conifers* are three excellent Wild Swan books by Gordon Gravett of 'Pempoul' fame. These superb books show that the scenic part of our hobby is one of the fastest-moving sectors at the moment.

Done in a Day: Easy Weathering and Detailing Projects by Pelle Søeborg is a soft-back magazine-style book published in the USA. Contains 88 pages and over 235 colour photographs and diagrams. The contents include the weathering of locomotives and rolling stock, making wagon loads, painting and detailing locomotives and how to install DCC and sound in locomotives. This is one of a huge range of railway modelling books by Kalmbach. Available in the UK from www.modeljunction.info or www.spv.co.uk.

Railway modellers are blessed with a vast array of books to choose from, covering most topics in the hobby.

Older books can be picked up at preserved railways and specialist second-hand bookshops and can be sources of inspiration.

Crowood's growing range of modelling books covers scenery making, DCC, maintaining locomotives, making buildings and so on. For more information go to www.crowood.com.

DVDS

The *RightTrack* range of DVDs covers locomotive building, making buildings, laying trackwork, scenery, weathering, DCC and carriages. For more information go to: www.model-railway-dvd.co.uk.

The *RightTrack Layout Planning and Design* DVD by Paul Lunn and Paul Marshall-Potter covers practical layout design and building skills, taking the viewer from the sketchpad to a completed layout. The project layout is built in OO scale, but the considerations for layout design apply to other scales as well.

Model Rail magazine has an expanding selection of useful DVDs, including weathering, making scenery, creative modelling, using an airbrush and much more: www.model-rail.co.uk.

There are four model railway magazines regularly available in most newsagents and some supermarkets in the UK. In Europe, there are another dozen or so model railway magazines, while in the USA there are three main modelling magazines.

Weathering techniques are well catered for in both books and DVDs. In addition, there are numerous YouTube posts of how to undertake weathering.

WEBSITES

Throughout this book, I have listed various websites that will be useful to readers in order to expand their knowledge and skills. There are a vast number of model railway websites that have been set up. Some are better than others. The ones that suggested here are those known at the time of writing.

Various good modellers have their own inspirational websites and here is a list of just a few of my personal favourites:

- www.georgedentmodelmaker.blogspot.co.uk.
- www.iainrobinsonmodels.blogspot.co.uk.
- www.nevard.com.
- www.philsworkbench.co.uk.
- www.albionyard.wordpress.com.
- www.soeeborg.dk.

Increasingly, Facebook is being used extensively by railway modellers to engage others in the hobby.

Forums are not everyone's cup of tea, but they can be good ways to expand your knowledge. Try www.modelrailforum.com and www.rmweb.co.uk.

It is always worth visiting manufacturers' websites to see what information they have for beginners. Both the websites of Bachmann and Hornby feature useful information to assist those new to the hobby.

Websites that specialize in weathering include:

- www.modeltrainsweathered.com.
- the Humbrol website has some good weathering videos using its products (www.humbrol.com).
- there are a lot personal websites carrying information about the different ways to weather a model. One such example is www.model-railroad-infoguy.com/Weathering-model-trains.html.
- the Tamiya website contains various movies and descriptions on how to use its various products: www.tamiya.com/english/products/87080weathering/.

It is worth having copies of the main catalogues in order to familiarize yourself with what is available. Sometimes we wonder 'Does anyone make such and such?' and five minutes' research with catalogues usually provides the answer. Internet search engines are another good reference tool.

CATALOGUES

While some modellers are content to browse the Internet to see what products and 'bits and bobs' are available for their chosen scale, others like to look through catalogues. In addition to listing all locomotives, the catalogues list the many other products that will be needed to make a layout, such as track pins, point motors, track ballast, signals, buildings, road vehicles, figures and scenic products. Catalogues depict both new releases and existing products. Some of the most useful and comprehensive catalogues are:

• The Bachmann, Graham Farish and Hornby catalogues, which are usually updated each January. The Dapol catalogue is updated annually and covers N, OO and O scales. The Heljan catalogue covers both OO and O scale models.

• Gaugemaster's catalogue is 136 pages long and is a good introduction to the huge range of tools, scenics, figures, control systems, track, kits, rolling stock and paints that are available.

• For plastic kits of wagons and buildings plus a large range of model railway accessories, buildings, scratch-building materials and so on for most of the common scales, the Ratio/Wills catalogue is comprehensive. For track and other accessories, the Peco catalogue runs to over 100 pages. It includes products for numerous scales, including N, OO, HOm, 009 and O scales.

• For scenic, the following catalogues are very useful: Busch, Faller, Noch and Woodland Scenics.

There is arguably no need to buy every edition of a catalogue because some companies provide 'new releases' leaflets to supplement their existing catalogues.

USEFUL WEBSITE ADDRESSES

This list contains some of the main manufacturers' and retailers' website addresses. Some of these sites provide product catalogues and direct ordering facilities. This list just gives a flavour of the huge number of model railway websites that are now readily accessible for those who have a computer and an Internet connection.

4D Model Shop – details, architectural trees
www.modelshop.co.uk

Bachmann – expanding ranges in N, OO and OO9
www.bachmann.co.uk

Dapol – wagons, locos and building kits
www.dapol.co.uk

Deluxe Materials – adhesives for all tasks
www.deluxematerials.co.uk

DoubleO Scenics – growing range of quality scenic
http://doubleoscenics.weebly.com/

Elite Baseboards – modern baseboard constructors
www.elitebaseboards.net

Expo Tools and Drills
www.expotools.com

Gaugemaster – controllers, scenics and more
www.gaugemaster.com

Golden Valley Hobbies – huge choice of products
www.goldenvalleyhobbies.com

Hedgerow Scenics – lots of grass mats and more
www.hedgerowscenics.co.uk

Heljan – growing range in OO and O scales
www.heljan.dk

Hobbycraft – useful nationwide craft stores
www.hobbycraft.co.uk

Hornby – a household name
www.hornby.com

Model Junction (Slough) – importer of US products
www.modeljunction.info

Model Tree Shop – lots and lots of trees!
www.themodeltreeshop.co.uk

Peco, K & M, Model Scene, Ratio and Wills
www.peco-uk.com

Squires Tools
www.squirestools.com

Train Terrain – great variety of scenics
www.trainterrainmodels.co.uk

Treemendus – good-quality trees and scenics
www.treemendus-scenics.co.uk

WW Scenics – static grass specialists
www.wwscenics.co.uk

WHAT SCENIC PRODUCTS ARE AVAILABLE?

This list shows just some of the many products that are available for making different aspects of scenery on a layout. The number of scenic products available is huge and growing all the time. I first started to prepare this list for my own use in 2007. When I revisited it in late 2014, I doubled the information on it because there are now so many more manufacturers making scenics in the UK.

At the time of writing, the list is as complete as possible, but there are new products and manufacturers that have probably arrived on the scene since I prepared it. I apologize for any errors and omissions. Some of the products listed here are very similar, but they are listed so that if you cannot obtain the products from one company, you can try a different one.

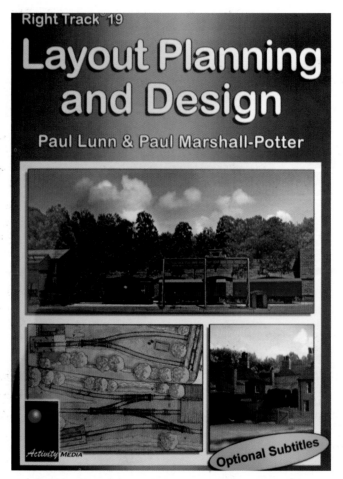

Cover of the Right Track Layout Planning and Design DVD.
PAUL MARSHALL-POTTER

Product	Company
Plaster-impregnated cloth	Busch, DoubleO Scenics, Gaugemaster, Geoscenics, Hornby, Noch, Peco, Scenic Express, Train Terrain and Woodland Scenics
Rocks	Cork Bark, DIY filler, ER Decor Hydrofibre, Noch hardfoam pieces and Woodland Scenics Hydrocal, moulds and Ready Rocks
Retaining walls	Busch, Dornaplus, ER Decor, Faller, Gaugemaster, Heki, Hornby, Kibri, Kingsway Models, Merkur, Noch, Ratio, Redutex, Scalescenes and Wills
Static grass fibres	Anita Decor, Busch, DoubleO Scenics, ER Decor, Faller, Heki, Javis, Noch, Woodland Scenics and WW Scenics
Static grass tools – electronic	DCC Automation, DoubleO Scenics, Faller, FMR, Green Scene, Heki, Noch and WW Scenics
Static grass tools – manual	Gaugemaster, Noch and WW Scenics
Scatter materials	Anita Decor, Auhagen, Busch, ER Decor, Faller, Gaugemaster, Green Scene, Heki, Hornby Skale Scenics, K & M, The Model Tree Shop, Noch, Peco, Scenic Express, Treemendus, Woodland Scenics and WW Scenics
Tall grasses	Faller Premium Terrain Grasses, Heki Wild Gras, Hedgerow Scenics Unkempt Grasses, Hornby Skale Scenics, Silflor Grass Tufts, Noch Reed Assortment, Scale Link etched brass, and Woodland Scenics Field Grass; grass tufts and strips are available from miniNatur and Noch
Foliage/weeds/ hedging	Auhagen, Busch, Green Scene, Hedgerow Scenics, Heki, K & M, Noch, Train Terrain, Treemendus, Woodland Scenics and WW Scenics
Grass tufts and strips	Busch, Gaugemaster, Heki, Noch, Treemendus
Wild flowers	Busch wild lupins and forest meadow, Faller Premium natural blossoms and shrubs, Heki Wiesengras, Noch Laser-Cut Minis, Scale Link etched brass, Silflor Pasture with Flowers, Noch Profi Meadow Flora, Flowering Foliage
Cornfields	Busch and Noch

(continued overleaf...)   *(continued overleaf...)*

Ploughed fields	Auhagen and Busch
Grass mats	Auhagen, Busch, ER Decor, Faller, Gaugemaster, Hedgerow Scenics, Heki, Javis, Langmesser Modellwelt, miniNatur, Model Scene (a Czech company), The Model Tree Shop, Noch and Woodland Scenics
Bespoke trees	Ceynix and Treemendus
Trees	4D Model Shop, Anita Decor, Auhagen, Busch, ER Decor, Faller, Gaugemaster, Green Scene, Heki, K & M, The Model Tree Shop, Noch, Treemendus and Woodland Scenics
Figures	Aidan Campbell, Bachmann Scenecraft, Dart Castings, Hornby, Langley Models, Model Scene Montys, Noch and Preiser
Roads	Busch, ER Decor, Faller, Gaugemaster, Noch and Woodland Scenics
Back scenes	Bilteezi, Busch, Faller, Gaugemaster, ID Back Scenes, MZZ, Noch, Peco, Sceniking, Street Level Models and Townscene
Fences	Ancorton, Atlas, Bachmann Scenecraft, Busch, Faller, Gaugemaster, Hornby, Kibri, Model Scene, Noch, Peco, Preiser and Ratio
Laser-cut details	Ancorton, Metcalfe, Noch, Ten Commandments, True Textures and York Model Making
Signs	Fox Transfers, Hornby Skaledale, Howard Scenic Supplies, Gaugemaster, Model Railway Scenery, Sankey Scenics, Scalescenes, Station Signs, Ten Commandments, Tiny Signs and Trackside
Motor vehicles	Bachmann Scenecraft, Base Toys, Cararama, Classix, Corgi Trackside, EFE, Gaugemaster, Hornby Skale Autos, Lledo and Oxford Diecast
Working street lights	Beli Beco, Brawa, Busch, Express Models, Heljan, Kytes, Langley Models, Patronics, Viessmann and Walthers
Interior lighting	Hornby Skale Lighting and doll's house lighting
Snow	Deluxe Materials makes a wide range of snow products. Faller, Geoscenics, Green Scene, Noch, Woodland Scenics and WW Scenics
Scenic adhesive	Deluxe Materials Scenic Spray Glue, extra-hold unscented hairspray, PVA from DIY stores, Treemendus Scenefix Glue, Woodland Scenics Scenic Cement and WW Scenics Premier FTG; all the major scenic manufacturers produce their own adhesives too

INDEX

RELATED TITLES FROM CROWOOD

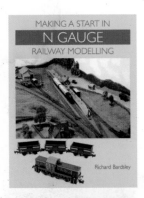

Making a Start in N Gauge Railway Modelling
RICHARD BARDSLEY
ISBN 978 1 84797 556 0
192pp, 300 illustrations

Planning, Designing and Making Railway Layouts in Small Spaces
RICHARD BARDSLEY
ISBN 978 1 84797 424 2
144pp, 130 illustrations

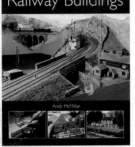

Making Model Railway Buildings
ANDY MCMILLAN
ISBN 978 1 84797 340 5
288pp, 620 illustrations

A Practical Introduction to Digital Command Control for Railway Modellers
NIGEL BURKIN
ISBN 978 1 84797 020 6
192pp, 400 illustrations

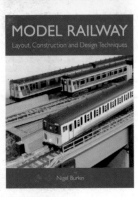

Model Railway Layout, Construction and Design Techniques
NIGEL BURKIN
ISBN 978 1 84797 181 4
192pp, 340 illustrations

Scenic Modelling
JOHN DE FRAYSSINET
ISBN 978 1 84797 457 0
160pp, 230 illustrations

In case of difficulty ordering, please contact the Sales Office:

The Crowood Press
Ramsbury
Wiltshire
SN8 2HR
UK

Tel: 44 (0) 1672 520320
enquiries@crowood.com
www.crowood.com